Purely Primitive
DOLLS

Purely Primitive
DOLLS

How to make simple, old-fashioned dolls

BARB MOORE

Photographs by Barb Moore and Impact Xpozures

STACKPOLE
BOOKS

Published by
STACKPOLE BOOKS
5067 Ritter Road
Mechanicsburg, PA 17055
www.stackpolebooks.com

Printed in the United States of America

10 9 8 7 6 5 4 3 2 1

First edition
Cover design by Wendy A. Reynolds

Library of Congress Cataloging-in-Publication Data

Moore, Barb.
  Purely primitive dolls : how to make simple, old-fashioned dolls / by Barb Moore. — First edition.
    pages cm
  ISBN 978-0-8117-1351-1
1. Rag doll making. I. Title.
  TT175.M65 2014
  745.592—dc23
                                    2014005631

Contents

Introduction

My name is Barb Moore, but most people know me as The Primitive Oswald. I have been creating primitive dolls and goods for many, many years. As a self-taught artist I have never taken any art classes or even a sewing class. I don't know how to read a pattern nor have I ever created a pattern or used one.

I enjoy designing all my own dolls and goods. I know that when someone buys one of my creations they'll have a piece of my heart in their home. Nothing warms my heart more than putting a smile on someone's face with one of my dolls.

My name, The Primitive Oswald, came from my dog. Oswald is my mini dachshund, and he is either sitting right next to me or he is in my lap. He watches me create almost every day and I love him to pieces. When my creations started selling I needed a name for myself. I wanted something unusual and something people would remember . . . the answer was sitting in my lap! So The Primitive Oswald was born.

I am a stay-at-home mom and I am by no means crafty. I tried that and found myself getting frustrated trying to create things just like others were making. I finally realized that crafting wasn't my thing, even though I enjoy creating. So I tried my hand at creating what I love—primitive dolls. There was no one more surprised than me to find that I had a knack for it. When people purchased my creations it gave me the confidence to keep on designing.

Now I want to share this with you and give you the tools you need to find a side of yourself you might never have recognized. Even if you only create primitive dolls for your own home you will be proud to know that you made them yourself. Every stitch was stitched with love, a treasure to be handed down, created with your very own hands.

CHAPTER 1

What Is Primitive Design?

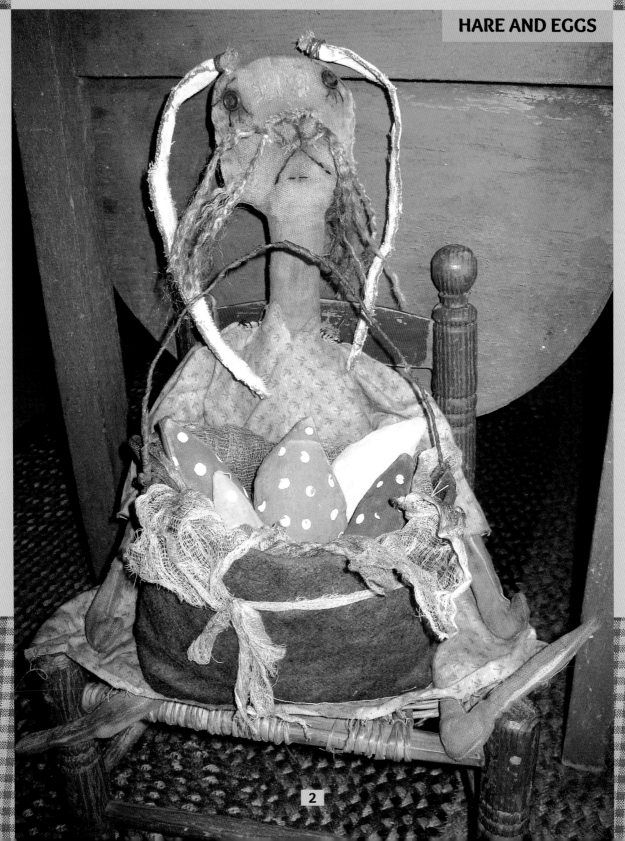

HARE AND EGGS

Have you ever seen decorations for homes that look to be years and years old? Have you ever held something in your hands and wondered about the history behind it?

Maybe you wanted to buy a primitive doll but found they were quite expensive. Maybe you wished you could make them for yourself but you had no idea where to start. Primitive design uses these reminders of the past to decorate and use in your home. My primitive art makes me feel like I am keeping the past alive and displaying treasures from years ago.

What is primitive? Simply put, primitive is when something looks old and well-used, simple and unsophisticated. Primitives are usually distressed and a bit worn around the edges. Primitive dolls, an important part of the world of prims, are handmade dolls—dolls made with simple techniques, simple materials, and hand-drawn designs. The bodies and clothes are often discolored (prim artists call it grunged), tattered, and torn. Clothing is frayed and unfinished, with a homespun charm you will find nowhere else. Prims tug at your heart. I love everything about primitive style and the details in the design. Primitives add charm to any home.

Think of days long ago when the man had to make everything for his family. He built the home and made everything inside—all the furniture, and everything needed to live, all completely handmade. People then used dyes from vegetables to make paint and milk paint to give color to their cabinets and furnishings. The wife sewed their clothing, using homespun and calico fabrics. Everything they used was simple and they couldn't afford any extras that came from the store—even if there was a general store close by.

Picture a daughter asking her mother to make her a doll to hold and love. Mother would make these dolls using scraps of fabrics from the clothes she made for her family and stuff them with rags, lumpy and bumpy. Maybe the dolls had hand-drawn faces, or maybe they had no face at all. I am sure that these dolls were loved to pieces.

Some might confuse antique style with primitive style. Primitive is in no way antique. Primitive means those things that haven't been restored, the old, old items left in their original state. In the olden days, items were made to withstand time and use and last through the years. A hand-carved wooden bowl a husband made for his wife, a cupboard to hold their tin dishes and sacks of flour and sugar—these were made to last. If a repair was needed, a scrap piece of tin was used to make a patch or repair.

Primitive dolls are huge in the world of primitive design. If you know someone who decorates their home in the primitive style you can rest assured they have primitive dolls. Even if you don't decorate primitive, one of these dolls is sure to speak to your heart. These dolls are conversation pieces as well as works of art.

Every artist has a different style: some styles are simple, some can be silly, some have a more country look, and some can be extreme primitive, which means they look extremely tattered and torn and well-loved. There are theme dolls: angels and Santas, Uncle Sams and scarecrows, dolls for the spring with a garden theme.

Primitive goods are also very common in a primitive home; you might find handmade vegetables, crows, or flowers. They all have one thing in common: they are handmade from fabric and are grunged. You will find lots of these dolls and other items online at primitive websites, in the back of most primitive magazines, and you can buy them from the online auction sites.

Be careful when purchasing primitive dolls. A real folk art doll will be one of a kind, signed and dated by the artist. There are companies who make large quantities of primitive dolls; these are made on an assembly line and are not true artist dolls. And remember that there is a big difference in a one-of-a-kind doll and a doll made from a pattern. Pattern dolls are wonderful, but they are another artist's design that you copy.

If you have seen primitive dolls and were sure that you could never make one yourself, I understand. I thought the same thing. It looked so hard and complicated and I was sure I needed to take sewing classes.

But I am here to show you that no classes are needed. I will show you step by step how to create a primitive doll and give you tips so the doll you create will be your very own style and not someone else's design. There is something special about creating your own dolls. That doll will be your own, and it will hold a piece of your heart. I will teach you how to take an idea, put it to paper, then to fabric, and lastly to reality—a doll you will be proud of.

Remember that there is no right or wrong way to do this. I will give you suggestions and tips to use as you learn the techniques. Then you will find a way that works for you. So come along with me into a whole new world of drawing, sewing, grunging (giving an aged appearance)—and find a piece of yourself you never knew existed.

Prairie doll with clothespin baby

CHAPTER 2
The Art of Designing Primitive Dolls

MISS HONEY BEE

When I decide to design a new doll, I look around for inspiration. I never know what that will be or when it might happen, so I always carry with me a small pad of paper and a pencil. I never know just when an inspiration will come.

For instance, one day I was sitting outside on my deck thinking about a design for a new doll. I was trying to come up with something new and a pesky bee wouldn't go away. So I was inspired to design a doll with a bee on her shoulder. I created a net out of wire and cheesecloth and a stick from my backyard; I added an old jar with a honey label on it.

You might find inspiration from one of my designs or from people you meet. Whatever you find that touches your heart can become a design for a doll, whether it be the doll's face or what she holds in her arms.

Here's all you need to get started. Find yourself a spiral notebook, a pad of paper, scrap copy paper—any blank paper will do—and a pencil. Let's draw!

Put it on paper

When you think about the kind of doll that appeals to you what comes to mind? Maybe a doll that appears to have been found in an old trunk in Granny's attic? Or maybe you would like to create something for a season, let's say spring or summer.

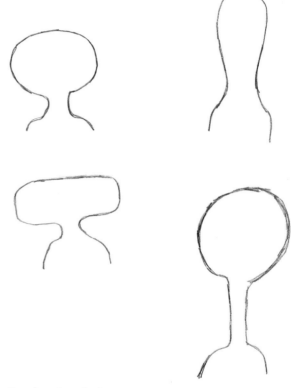

Head and neck shapes

1. With paper and pencil in hand, first draw the head: round, oblong, long and skinny—the choice is yours. Any shape is fine because there is no wrong or right in primitive design. If you don't feel comfortable the first time drawing freehand you can use a small plate or other object as a template. But remember: unless you are an expert sewer you most likely won't be able to follow exactly the lines when it comes time to sew the doll together. I am not an expert sewer so I can't follow the lines, but that is okay. Draw a head shape that appeals to you.

2. Next, draw the neck: long and skinny, or short and wide. The size of the neck should be in relation to the size of the head. I have made plenty of rather small-headed dolls with long skinny necks. But remember that the neck must support the head, so if you design a large head and want a long neck as well, make the neck wide enough to hold the head.

3. Next are the shoulders. Here, again, the choice is yours. The shoulder shape will depend on how skinny or wide you want your doll to be. Draw the shoulders of your doll.

4. After you draw the curve of the shoulders, draw straight down. This will determine the length of the body. Once more, the choice is yours. Do you want a big doll or a small one? Make that decision now.

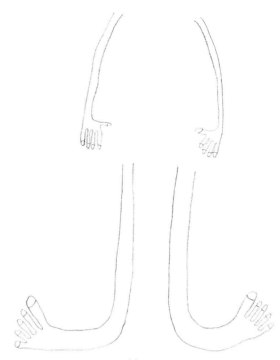

Garden doll, arms and legs

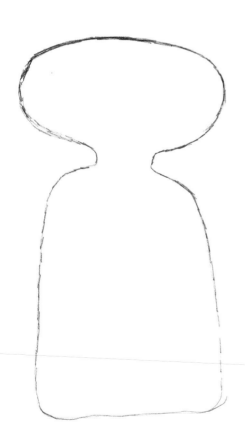

Granny doll, head and body shape

5. Then draw a straight line across the bottom of the doll's body. Now you have your basic doll shape.

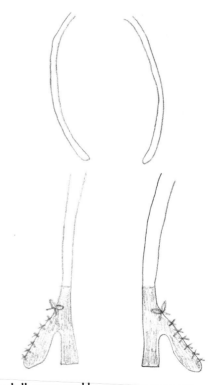

Granny doll, arms and legs

6. Next draw the arms and legs. The arms should start at her shoulders and come down to the bottom of her body. The width is up to you: if your doll is skinny, then make her arms skinny. If she is a big, hefty doll, you might draw wider arms.

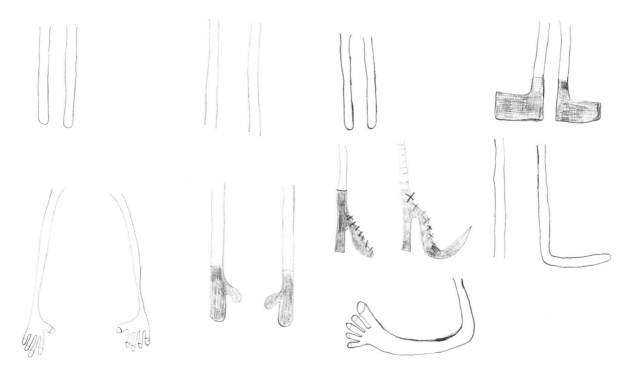

Arm styles: simple arms, open ended (extreme prim), hands with fingers, mittened hands

Leg styles: simple legs, boy boots, granny boots, witch boots, open ended (extreme prim), long feet, feet and toes

7. If you'd like to start easy, round off the ends of the arms for hands. Or you can get more creative and draw a hand that looks like a mitten. Or if you are up to the challenge, you can draw hands with fingers. The choice is yours.

8. Next come the legs. Start at the bottom of the body. Draw in some legs. As you did with the arms, consider the size and width of your doll. I happen to like extra long legs on my dolls, but any width is fine. Draw what is appealing to you.

9. Last of all are the feet. You have plenty of choices for feet styles. You can go simple with rounded ends or get more creative. Here are a few of my designs I have done throughout the years. In Chapter 3 we will talk about drawing shoes, boots, fingers, and toes. You can get inspiration from my drawings to create your own.

You now have a paper drawing of your doll. Take the time to make any changes now before you draw it onto the fabric.

Garden doll, finished drawing

Granny doll, finished drawing

Fabrics for the Doll's Body

BLOOM

There are many types of fabrics to choose from for your doll. If you have never been to a fabric store, take a trip to see what is available. For those not familiar with fabric stores, it can be overwhelming. But don't worry about all those fabrics—I will guide you through your choices.

My fabric of choice: painter's drop cloth

- The most popular choice is muslin. It comes in two colors, unbleached and bleached, and a variety of thread counts or weights (thicknesses), and a range of prices. Muslin is loosely woven cotton, and it is great for many different uses in doll making. The more expensive it is per yard the more weight or thickness it has.

- Next most popular is osnaburg. It is a cotton fabric with a nubby, rough feel. You can usually find it with the utility fabrics in fabric stores. It also comes bleached or unbleached. I like using osnaburg because of its texture.

- Next is natural ticking. This is also a utility fabric and it is heavy and thick. Most ticking has some color of stripes on it; natural ticking has no stripes. Because of its thickness, it will stand up well to the whole process of primitive doll making. This was my choice until I found something very unusual.

- Here is my favorite fabric to make my creations with: painter's tarp. It is just what you think: a tarp that painters lay down to protect the floors when they paint. It is very heavy and thick and can stand up to anything you put it through while making your doll: grunging, painting, and even sanding. It holds up well for my extreme primitive dolls with all the tatters I put on them. You can find painter's tarps at any home improvement store. They come in a variety of sizes and shapes. Painter's tarps are inexpensive for the amount of fabric you get so if you choose to use them you will get the most bang for your buck. A 9' x 12' tarp will make many dolls and primitive pieces. I make all my dolls and primitive goods with these. Pricewise you just can't beat it.

- But you can think even more outside the box. Old cotton sheets or pillowcases, even a bed skirt you are no longer using will work, as long as they are a natural cream color or white. I even buy cotton skirts or tablecloths at thrift stores for my dolls.

Fabric you buy at a fabric store is sold by the yard and the size doll you make will determine the amount you need to buy. Remember when you are planning your doll that you must make two sides, a front and a back. You will fold the fabric in half so there are two layers. And don't forget you will have two arms and two legs—that means four legs and four arms to cut out.

I suggest two to four yards of fabric for the doll's body, just to be safe. The amount you need will depend on the size of the doll. A small doll (12"–20") won't require nearly as much fabric as a larger doll, so keep that in mind as you shop. Sometimes fabric stores have sales and if you find a good price on your favorite fabric, consider buying the whole bolt. It is nice to have extra on hand for other projects you might have in mind. Extra fabric is also nice if you make a mistake or change your mind and want to start over. I usually buy two or three painter's tarps at a time so that I never have to make a quick trip to buy more if I unexpectedly run out or have an inspiration that I want to work on at once.

Experiment with all the different kinds of fabric that you think might work and use what you feel comfortable with. Personally, I prefer a heavier fabric, but you may not: you might prefer muslin or osnaburg.

CHAPTER 4

Putting Your Drawing onto Fabric

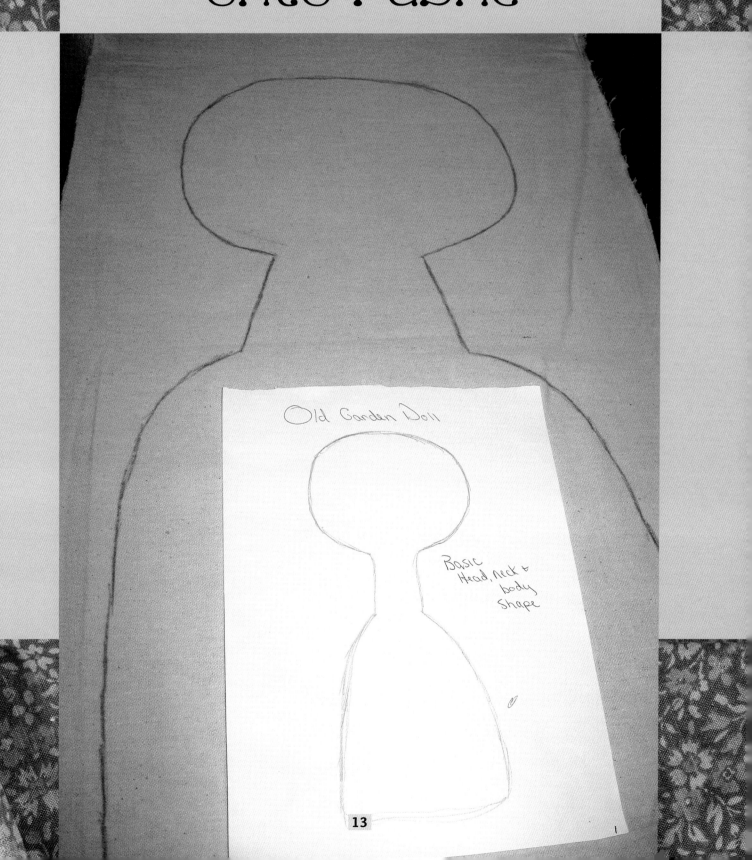

Old Garden Doll

Basic
Head, neck &
body
shape

13

ow you have your very own drawing of the doll you want to create and you have chosen the fabric you want to make her out of. So let's get started transferring your drawing from the paper onto the fabric.

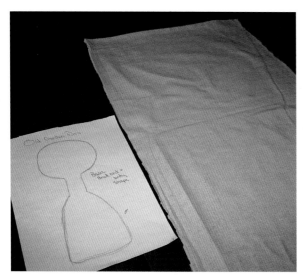

1. Spread your fabric out onto a large workspace such as your kitchen table. Fold the fabric in half. This is so that you will have both a front and back for your doll. (Note: You will always have to fold your fabric in half with any doll or doll accessory that you make so that you will have a front and a back.)

   Place your drawing of your doll next to you. You might want to cut out your drawing to use as a pattern to trace around. You can do that, but I skip that step. The doll makers of old didn't have patterns and they just forged ahead. I think that freehand drawing gives a more primitive look. With your pencil, draw your doll onto the fabric. Please remember: there is no wrong way to do this, so start wherever you like. I like to start with the head.

2. Starting at the top of your fabric, leaving a two-inch border at the top and on all sides,

draw the head. Leave the opening for the neck. The size head you draw will be the actual size of her head so take your time on this step. This side of the fabric will be on the inside of the doll, so if you need to erase and start over, don't worry.

When you like the size and shape of the head, move down and draw the neck. Remember that the width you draw is the actual width of her neck.

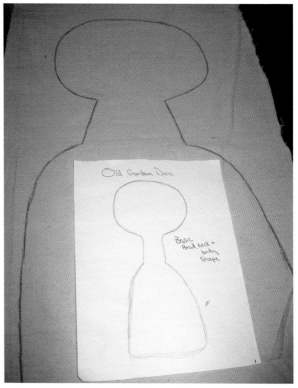

3. Now move across to draw the shoulders. These should be a bit wider then her head. Then draw straight down for the body, and draw a line across the bottom of her body to finish it off. Don't worry if your lines are crooked—remember this is freehand drawing. This is what primitive is all about! Remember the shape and size are what you have envi-

sioned so only you can decide if it is right or wrong. The whole idea here is for you to create your own style doll, and that includes her shape and size. You can't mess this up because it is your design.

4. Next we will work on the arms and legs. Lay more of your chosen fabric out on the table, remembering to fold it in half for a front and back side. Leave a two-inch border all around the arms and legs. Let's start with the arms. The width depends on the length and width of your doll, but you want the arm length to be from shoulder to bottom of body. You can measure if you like, but freehand is just what primitive is all about. Make two arms with rounded ends, open ends, mittens, or even with fingers—it is your choice.

You can look at my drawings to get an idea of what fingers might involve. This is a little more complicated but with some practice you can do it. Make sure to leave enough space between the fingers for cutting and sewing. Toes are done almost the same way; look at my drawing of feet and toes. When I do fingers and toes I like to paint their fingernails and toenails. Do this when the doll is completely finished. You can use either regular nail polish or paint. If I make a black doll I usually paint the nails either white or some other bright color. If I do just a straightforward grungy doll out of a light-colored fabric, any color will work.

Draw the legs, then move right or left to make the foot, then the toes. This isn't hard but you need to have patience. Remember you can always erase if you need to. Look at my drawings for ideas, or come up with your own designs. Leave a two-inch border around arms, fingers, legs, and feet.

There you have it: your basic doll design on fabric.

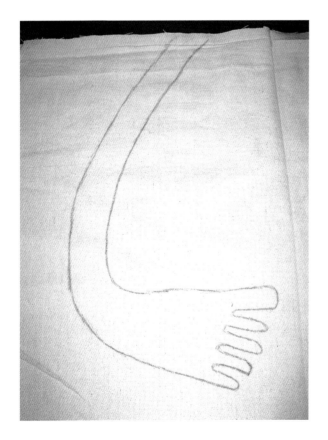
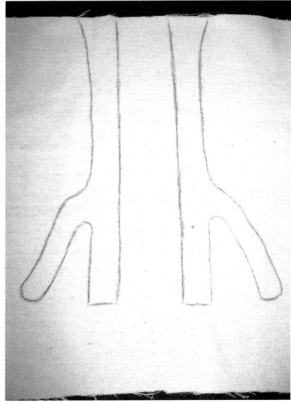

CHAPTER 5
Cutting and Sewing

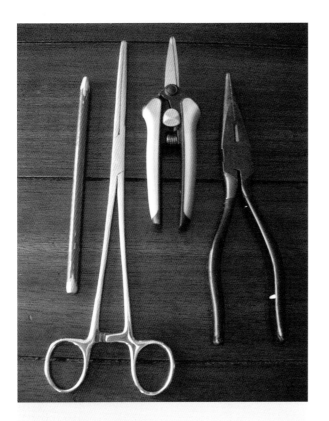

Cutting

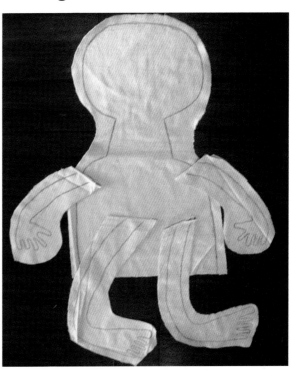

MATERIALS AND SUPPLIES

Sewing machine. It does not have to be an
  expensive one; mine is 20 years old and
  I have no idea how to use many of the
  different features. If you plan to buy a new
  machine for these projects I suggest you
  go to a fabric store and ask for suggestions. Explain that you are a beginner and
  want a simple machine. I only use it to do
  a straight stitch, so you can see just how
  simple the machine can be.
Scissors. Two kinds, one for heavy cutting
  and a smaller one for trimming. Don't
  skimp on these: buy good quality scissors
  and they will last. And never use your fabric
  scissors to cut anything but fabric. That
  will ruin them.
Needle nose pliers.
Hemostat. Buy a large one.
Pencil with a broken tip.

First, cut out your doll body and her arms and
legs. Remember to leave a generous two-inch
border around all the pieces. Don't throw away
the scraps of leftover material; save them in a bag
for later.

Sewing

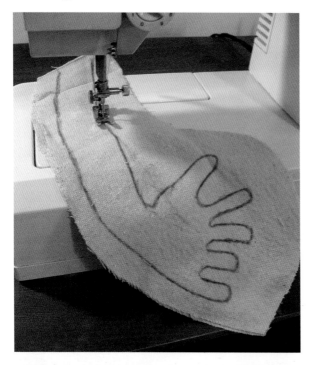

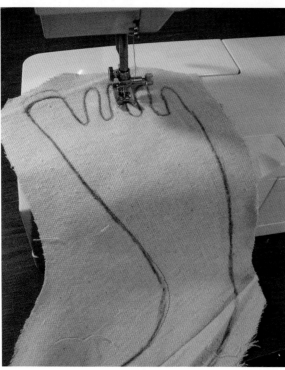

and legs. Be especially careful around the curves in the head, shoulders, between the fingers and toes, and anywhere else you have a curve. Do not sew the bottoms closed: leave the bottom of the body, arms, and legs open for stuffing. Remember, your sewing doesn't have to be perfect. Imperfection is what we are striving for.

Trimming

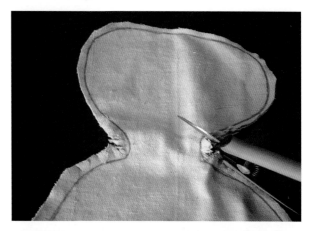

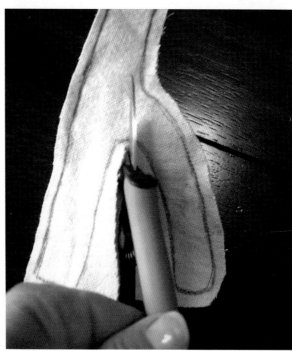

With your sewing machine, stitch around your drawing following the lines you drew, using a straight stitch to sew the pieces together. Start at the bottom of one side of the body and stitch slowly. Do the same with each piece of the arms

Turning

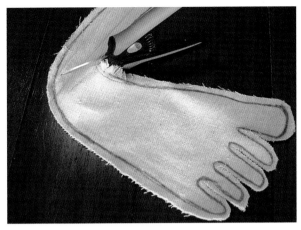

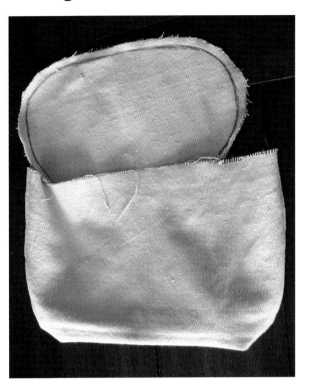

Next you will trim the excess fabric away. Be very careful with this. Take your time cutting along the stitching line, leaving about ¼ inch or so seam allowance. As you trim the angles and curves, leave a little more of an allowance because you will need to take tiny snips, cutting into that curve, getting as close to the stitching as you can without cutting through it. Look at the picture to better understand this step.

Take all of the scraps and put them with the others you saved. Stockpile these scraps because they come in handy.

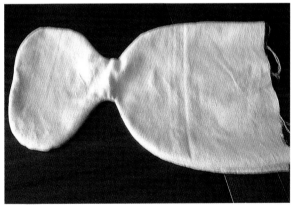

1. Now it is time to turn everything right side out.

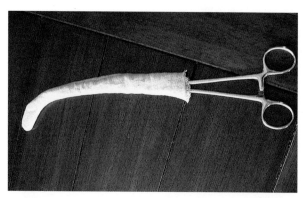

2. Using the hemostat or pliers, carefully grab the fabric and, little by little, start turning each piece right side out. When each piece is turned, poke the broken-tip pencil or hemostat inside to smooth out all the edges, corners, and seams. This makes your pieces easier to paint and grunge.

Now you have constructed all the pieces of your doll. Are you ready to make her look primitive? The next chapter will get you started.

Grunging and Baking, Painting and Sanding

ow that you have your doll turned right side out it is time for the grunging stage. I grunge in two stages.

MATERIALS AND SUPPLIES

Old cookie sheet

Tinfoil

Old soup pot or any old deep pot

Instant coffee. The cheapest you can find is just fine.

Cinnamon (ground)

Sandpaper (#24 extra coarse)

Acrylic paint, flat black (brands I like are Apple Barrel, Ceramcoat, and Folk Art.)

Old small paintbrush

Old wooden spoon, or any old spoon

Oven

Old plastic container (Cool Whip size or smaller)

What makes a primitive doll a prim is its old appearance. Careworn, loved to death, many years of use—that is the look we want. Old furniture or vintage fabrics—it is the many years of being used and being worn that give them character. We are creating a new doll but we want it to look old, and well used, and well loved, so we have to do something to give it this old, worn character. In the world of prims, we call it grunging.

Grunging, stage 1

1. Fill your old pot with 4 cups of water; bring it to a rolling boil. Add about 2 cups of instant coffee and let it boil for a few minutes. Add

about 1 teaspoon of ground cinnamon, stir it in well, and let it boil for a few minutes. You can adjust these measurements of the coffee and cinnamon according to the amount you will need for each piece. If you are making a small doll then make less solution. Be careful with the cinnamon: you don't want the solution to be too thick. It should be about the consistency of milk.

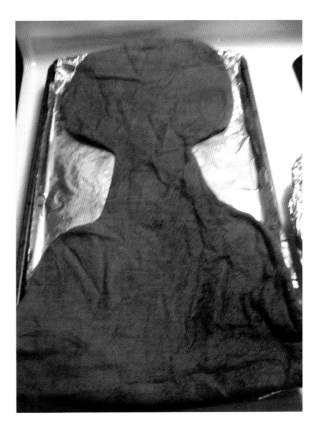

2. Now here's the tricky part. Test the mixture to see how dark the liquid will turn your doll. Put one of the arms or legs into the pot and push it down with your spoon to soak up the mixture. Stir it around to see how dark your doll piece becomes. If you are satisfied, then you're good to go. If not, add more instant coffee, stir it around, and let boil for a few more minutes.

3. Once you have achieved the darkness you like, put in the rest of the doll pieces. I usually leave her there for about 30 minutes. Be sure that the solution is hot: this helps the fabric accept the grunge solution better. Turn off the burner and let the pieces soak until the grunging solution is cool.

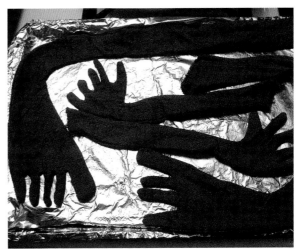

4. Then squeeze the grunge solution out of your doll and lay the pieces flat on a tinfoil-covered cookie sheet. Be careful that you don't overlap any of the pieces.

5. Baking. You might have to do the baking step in shifts, as if you were baking cookies. Turn your oven on to warm or the lowest setting, and let the pieces bake until they are dry. This can take anywhere from 20 to 30 minutes, depending on the type of fabric. Thinner fabric will dry faster. Watch carefully so that the doll doesn't burn. The baking process helps turn the fabric doll an even darker color. When it is dry pull it out and let it cool. After she has been baked, if I don't feel she is dark enough, I grunge and bake her again.

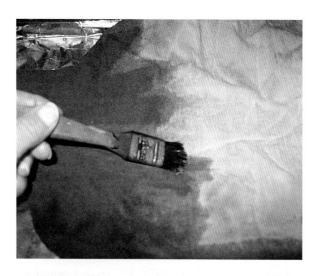

6. Painting. Squeeze a tablespoon or two of black paint into the plastic container and add some hot water to thin it out. How black you want your doll determines how much water you add. The more water you add the lighter the paint will be. If you add too much water your doll will be gray; if it looks too light, just add more paint to your mixture and try again.

Note: You can leave your dolls just grungy and not paint them—the process is the same except you skip the painting step.

Be certain to get paint into all the edges and all the seams. Flip her over, paint the back side, and then flip her over again. Put her back on the cookie sheet and into the oven until she is dry.

You can flip the parts over a few times if you want to, but I never remember to do this. If you forget like I do, then you will have a definite front and back side to your doll. The side that is against the cookie sheet will be lighter when dry.

When your doll comes out of the oven she could be very stiff. That is good—you want her to be stiff. The next step (sanding) will take care of this stiffness. If it is a hot summer day, you can let your doll dry outside in the sun instead of in the oven. A hot breezy day is perfect for grunging. I sometimes string up a temporary clothesline and hang all the doll pieces from it. Be sure to let all the pieces dry completely before continuing.

7. Sanding. When all parts are completely dry it's time for sanding. This is a great step to do outside. Work on a flat surface. Give each part a good sanding. If you happen to put a hole through the fabric, don't worry—that is the primitive style. You might even want that! I like to do a heavier sanding to the face for a more worn look.

Save the remainder of your grunging solution for later. Put the pot in the refrigerator where it will stay good for a few days. We will be using the solution again for your doll's second grunging and for her clothes. If there isn't much solution left, don't worry because you can always make more. Every time you use it, make sure that you put it back on the stove and heat it up before you put the pieces in. Fabric grunges better when the solution is warm.

CHAPTER 7
Stuffing Your Doll

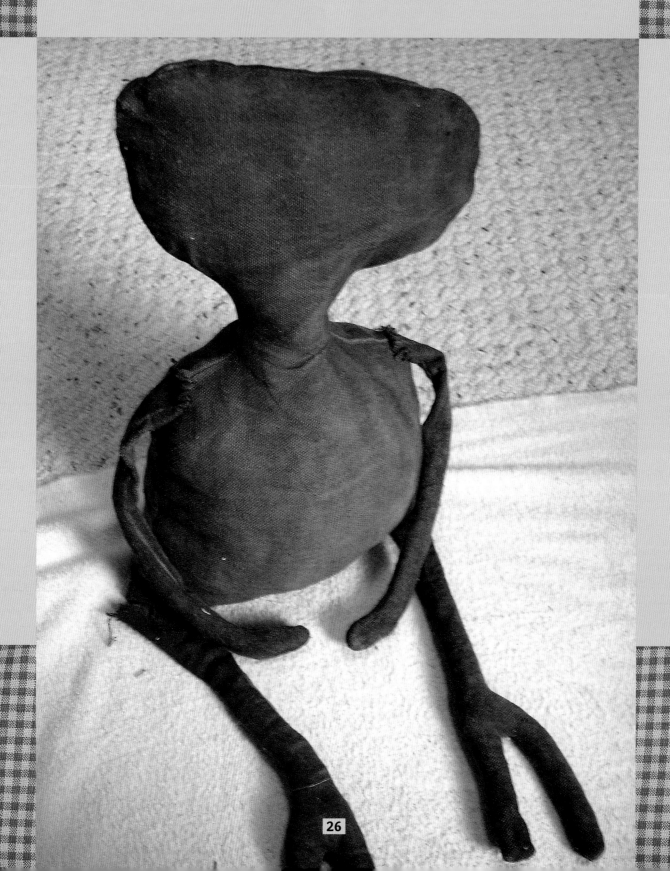

26

Kinds of stuffing

MATERIALS AND SUPPLIES

DMC floss. This can be found at any fabric store. You will need black, creams, shades of red, and any other shades that you like. In fact, you will never have too many colors. You will eventually want dark gray because that color works well for prim-pinching noses and mouths. I buy all the autumn colors and all different shades of mustards and creams.

Stuffing

Needle for hand sewing. You will need a needle with a sharp point and a large eye for sewing with heavy thread.

Hemostat

Thimble

There are many types of stuffing you can use. For my dolls, I only stuff with rags because it gives my dolls that old lumpy and weighty feel that adds to their primitive charm. Remember, in the olden days they didn't have poly fill so they stuffed with whatever was around, often rags or scraps of fabric. Everybody I know saves me all their old clothes, linens, towels, bed sheets. Old socks are great to use for stuffing a long neck. I like to cut up the old rags as I go to the size I need as I stuff the doll.

And then there is poly fill. You can find this at any fabric store or craft store; some department stores may carry it. You can even choose to use a combination of both rags and poly fill. I save all my scraps from trimming the dolls, and I often use these scraps to stuff their arms and legs.

Time to stuff

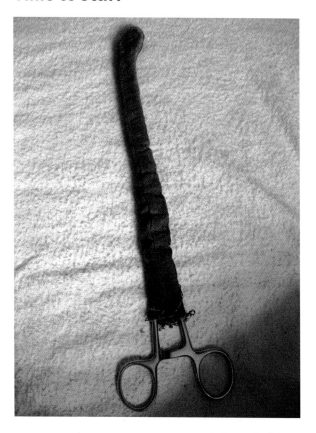

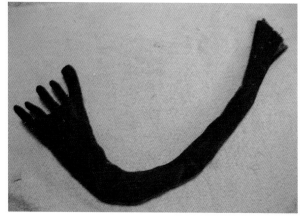

1. You will need your hemostat for this step. If you don't have a hemostat, you can use a long pencil. Start by stuffing the arms. Little by little, push your stuffing down to the end of the arm and keep adding until you have reached ¾ the way up the arm.
2. Stuff the legs the same way. If you poke a hole through the arm or leg, don't worry about it—this will give her even more character. You can either stuff loosely or stuff firmly; it all depends on the look that you want.

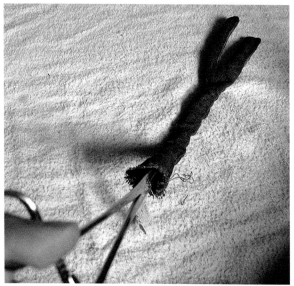

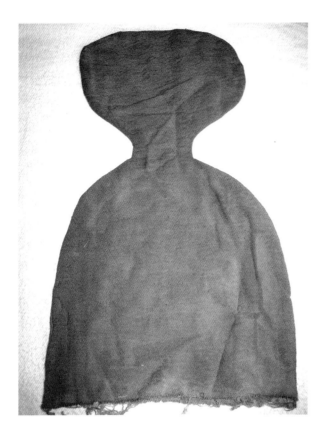

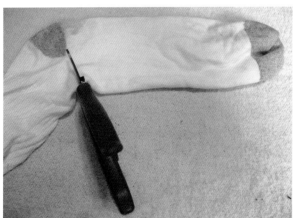

3. Now it's time to stuff the body. As you push the stuffing up into the head, make sure to get it all around the head shape. This is one piece you should stuff firmly. Fill in the center of the head and slowly add the stuffing down into the neck. Hold up your doll and if the head stays erect, you are ready to stuff the body cavity. If the head does not stay erect, then carefully keep pushing in more stuffing with the hemostat until her head stays up. This is where old socks come in handy: they are perfect for stuffing a neck. If by chance you poke a hole in one of the seams you will have to repair it because you don't want her to come apart or the seams to unravel. After she is stuffed, be sure to repair that seam from the outside. It might look a little messy now, but after you do the second grunging it won't show too much. And remember that this doll is prim, so anything goes.

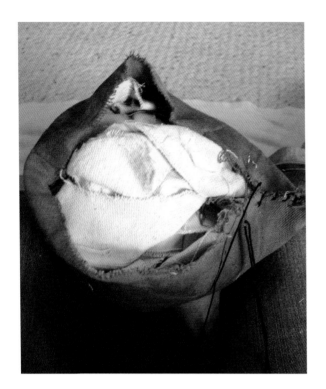

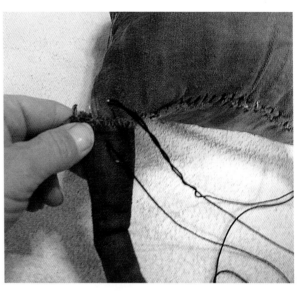

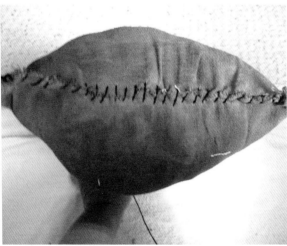

4. Sewing her closed. When she is all stuffed
   to your satisfaction, it's time to sew up the
   bottom. The color of floss that you use for
   this step depends on the color of your doll.
   Use three strands of the floss and thread your
   needle. Knot the end and sew together the
   bottom of your doll. Don't worry about being
   neat—this is one time where sloppy is just
   fine.

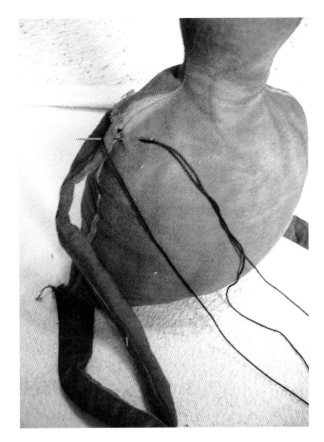

Remember you can stuff your doll loosely or you can stuff her firmly; the choice is yours. I do both—it depends on the style of doll. If it is a prairie doll then I stuff looser. Prairie dolls are made to look like children's toys and a loosely stuffed doll will be floppy and huggable and look like it was well loved by a child long ago. When I make a theme doll, such as a seasonal doll, I stuff firmly so that the doll will hold its shape.

Now you have your doll's body ready to go and we are ready for the fun part. The next chapter will help you bring life to your creation.

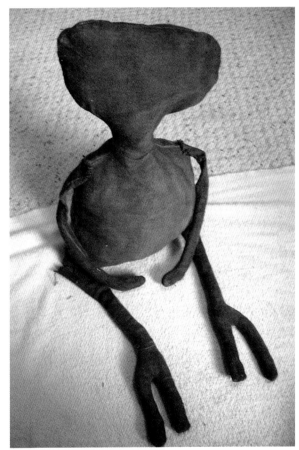

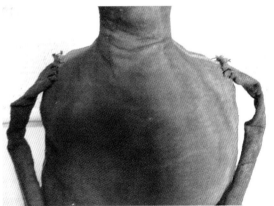

5. You can insert the legs into the body now or sew them onto the body after the body is closed up: that is up to you, either way works. Decide where you would like to place her arms and using the same floss, attach her arms to the body. Remember, when you stitch the arms on it doesn't have to be perfect. Using a black floss looks extra prim on a grungy doll. I strive for the primitive handmade look.

CHAPTER 8

Creating the Face

GARDEN FLOWER

Here is where we bring your creation to life. I love this part because it is so much fun trying to reproduce what I have drawn on paper.

Draw the face on paper

Granny doll face: fabric and floss knot eyes with rusty wire glasses; wide prim pinched nose; double pinched mouth with red homespun fabric; flax hair

Garden doll face: flower petal hair, button eyes, floss nose and mouth, blushing cheeks

You will need to have your drawing of your doll as your guide. The first step is to decide what you would like her to look like. There are so many different styles of faces and different ways to make a face—the possibilities are endless. I'll tell you how I proceed.

I always start with the eyes. In my drawings, I show you many different eye styles, but these are not the only possibilities. If you have another idea, that is great—use your own design. (Note: If you would rather draw your facial features on instead of sewing them on, you will do this after the next grunging and sanding step.)

Eyes: floss, fabric squares with floss knots, buttons, floss X's, triangle for pumpkins, knots, pencil drawn

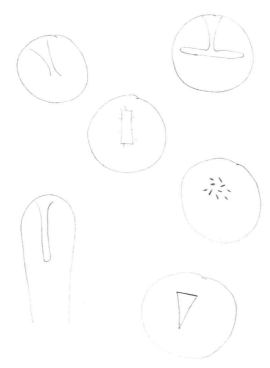

Noses: prim pinched, wide pinched, fabric, floss stitches, drawn, triangle for pumpkin

Now draw the nose. I have given many different styles and looks for noses, but you can design your own. Remember: this is your doll; you are the designer.

The mouth is next: there are so many different ways to do mouths. It all depends on just how prim you want your doll to look. Look at my drawings for ideas or create your own. Maybe you saw a doll in a magazine or in an antique store that left a lasting impression on you. Use that doll as inspiration.

Putting the face on the doll
Eyes
BUTTON EYES

Once you have the face designed on paper, it is time to put that face on your stuffed doll. Let's say you want button eyes. Find two old buttons; I like to use different sizes of mismatched buttons. Place the buttons on her face to decide just where you want to attach them. Remember this is primitive and they do not have to be level with each other or spaced any certain way. Anything goes!

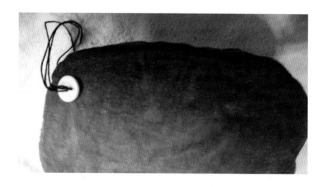

Mouths: knots, straight stitch floss, fabric squares, floss stitches, double pinched, prim pinched, fabric with knots, drawn

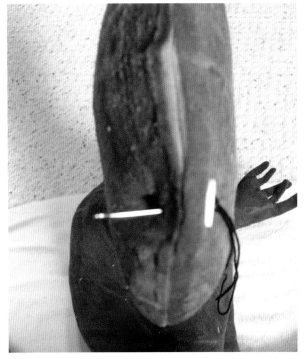

Thread your needle with three strands of black DMC floss and knot the end. Sew the button in place by going from the back of the head through to the front, just like you would sew a button on a shirt. It might be hard to push all the way through the thickness of the head, so a thimble and needle nose pliers come in handy. Push the needle through using the thimble and grab the needle with the pliers as it comes out the opposite side. Attach both eyes this way. Go back and forth a few times through the button so it holds good and tight. Secure with a knot on the back side of her head.

Keep an eye open for buttons. If you come across a jar of old buttons in an antique shop or flea market, buy them. Save all your extra buttons too. Ask your mom or grandma if they have a button jar. Spread the word to friends that you are collecting old buttons. You will love what comes your way.

FABRIC AND KNOT EYES

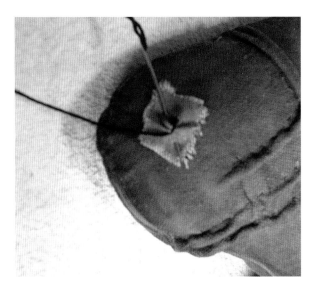

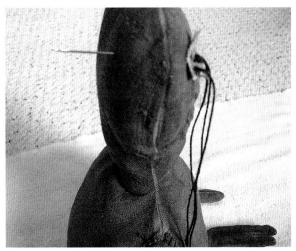

Another primitive eye style uses fabric with a knot in the center. Use little scraps of leftover fabric that you saved. Make a small square shape; the size will depend on how big or small you want her eyes to be. Thread your needle and knot the end of your thread. The size and style of knot depends on the look that you want. (You could even use a French knot if you want a fancier eye. I prefer a regular knot for my primitive dolls.) Start at the center of your square and carefully push your needle through and come out the back side of her head, then knot the thread on the back side. That is all there is to it: a simple knot and fabric scrap eye.

OTHER SIMPLE EYES

- Floss stitched eyes are fairly easy. Use three or more strands of cream color floss for horizontal stitches, then stitch vertical stitches on top of those with black floss.
- Or make fabric eyes by using squares or triangles which you attach with tiny stitches, around the outside of the shape, to hold the small piece in place.
- Simple floss X's are super easy.
- Tiny buttons with floss stitches all around the button (like on a Raggedy Ann doll) are also cute.
- You can add eyelashes by adding stitches above the button, using cream floss on a black doll and black floss on a grungy doll.

Nose

I will show you two different styles for the two dolls I am making.

FLOSS NOSE

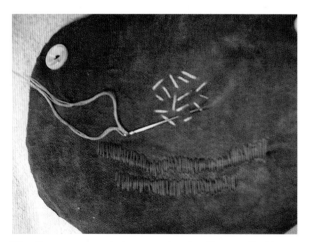

The first nose style is very simple. On my Garden Doll I used all six strands of a dark brown floss. Make small tiny stitches, your needle going in and

out without going all the way through to the back side, just picking up the face fabric. Tiny stitches this way and that—there should be no rhyme or reason or pattern to these stitches. When you have the amount you like, take the needle and thread all the way through to the back side and knot it.

PRIM PINCHED NOSE

The second nose style is on my Granny Doll. This is a bit trickier. The technique is called prim pinching and it takes some practice, but remember we don't want perfection in primitive dolls. For this style nose, match the floss color to the fabric color. Here I used dark gray floss, all six strands for strength.

Start at the top of the back side of the head, push the needle through slightly off center. Once through, carefully go back into the head and come out slightly off center about 1/4 inch away. Go in and out, back and forth, coming out on the opposite side and pulling the thread taut so the fabric puckers a little. Continue this way until you have the length of the nose you want. Then knot the thread by going through to the back side as before.

You can define the nose even more. When you have the nose length you want, take your needle and go to the side to create the wide part of the nose. You do the prim pinch sewing the same way, only to the side instead of up and down. When the nose is the width you want, knot the thread on the back side of the head.

FABRIC STUFFED NOSE

Garden Flower

You can use any kind of fabric, from painter's tarp to calico, and any pattern or color fabric, cut into any shape. Start with an oval shape for your first stuffed nose. Decide where you want it on the face. Match the floss to the nose fabric and make tiny stitches all around the piece. I leave a tiny opening and stuff the nose before I stitch it closed. This makes it stand out a bit from the face and I like the look.

Mouth

FLOSS MOUTH

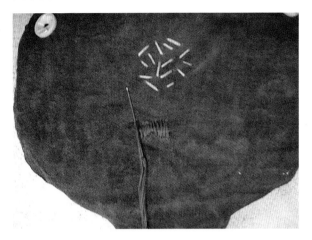

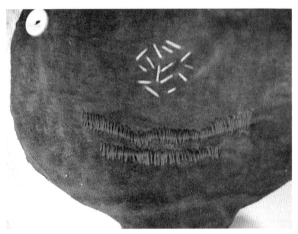

A floss smile is the simplest mouth. Choose a floss color you like and use all six strands of floss. Take tiny stitches in and out through the face fabric, not through to the back side. If you want a smile, start on one end and make stitches on an angle, then stitch in the same way back up to the opposite side of her face. For her bottom lip, do the same but make the bottom lip smaller. For a primitive look, I try hard to make my stitches uneven. This way and that way . . . think and stitch like a child and have fun.

You can make your doll's mouth wide so it looks like a big smile or you can make a tiny little mouth. You can make a wide open mouth and add floss teeth, a great idea if you are making a pumpkin doll.

Double prim pinched mouth

A more challenging mouth is called double prim pinched. This is just like the pinched nose. Your needle goes in and out, pulling the thread taut to make the fabric pucker. First form the top lip, then the bottom lip. Then take the thread all the way through to the back side and knot it as before.

For a real prim look, you can add red homespun to her mouth. Tear the fabric to the correct width and length. Be sure to make it wide enough to wrap around the pinched lips.

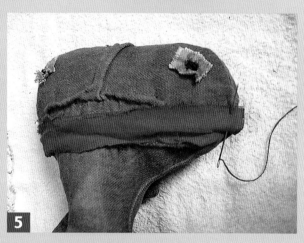

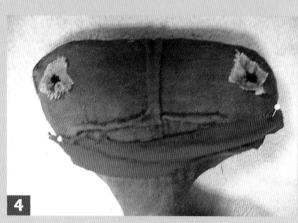

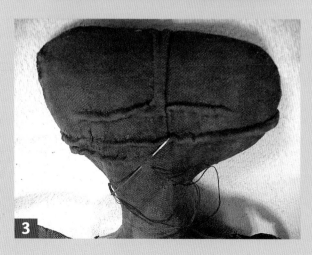

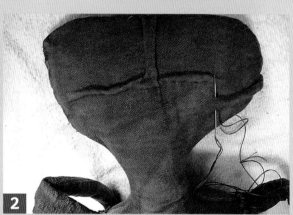

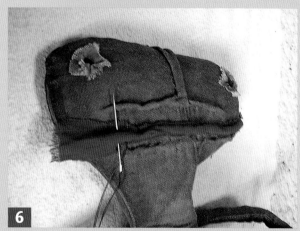

Then take tiny stitches using red embroidery floss. Poke your needle right through the pinched lip to securely attach the red fabric. Knot the thread at the end of the mouth.

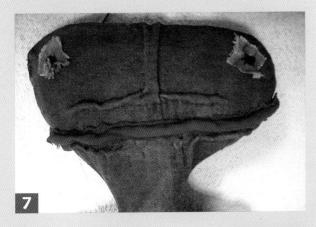

7

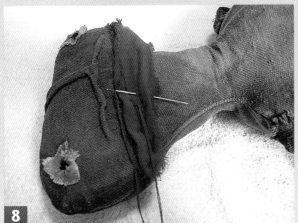

8

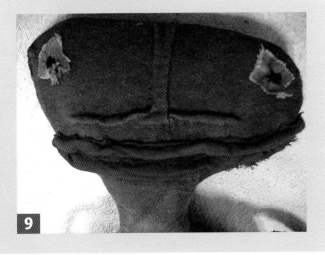

9

MORE MOUTH IDEAS

▥ For a very simple mouth, simply stitch a rectangular strip of red homespun in place.
▥ Use little black squares for a snowman mouth.
▥ Or just use black knots or just a straight line of your choice of color floss.

As you can imagine, the more you practice with your drawings the more ideas you will come up with. The idea here is to make your doll's facial features in your own way, a way that touches your heart, a doll that speaks to what you are feeling on the day you are creating her. You might even choose to do no face at all, maybe just sew a patch somewhere on her face. My faces depend on my mood—and if I am in a silly mood you can be sure my doll has some silly teeth!

Two Front Teeth

CHAPTER 9
Grunging, Stage Two

GRANNY

MATERIALS AND SUPPLIES

Grunging mixture

Tinfoil

Cookie sheet

Paintbrush

Cinnamon

Old paring knife

Sandpaper

Adding more age

We are now at the second stage of grunging. This is where your doll will take on the perfect primitive look.

1. You can use the coffee mixture you have in your old pot left over from before or you can make some new grungy solution. You can re-fresh it with more water, coffee, or cinnamon if you think you need to. Bring the mixture to a boil and let it boil until it is nice and thick, like honey. If it isn't thickening, add more cinnamon.

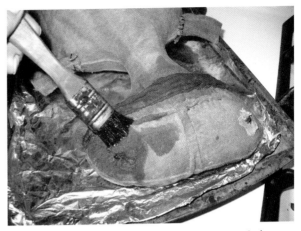

2. In the meantime, lay your doll on a tinfoil-covered cookie sheet. Turn the oven on to warm. Get your paintbrush and cinnamon. Once the mixture is thick, turn off the burner, dip your paintbrush into the mixture and scrape along the bottom of the pot. You want to find the thick stuff that is settled on the bottom. Brush this thick mixture all over your doll's face. Keep going back for more and paint it on until her face is completely cov-ered. Paint her neck, the upper body, arms, and legs.

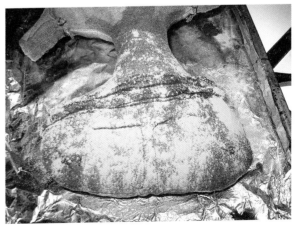

3. Once you have her covered with this grung-ing mixture sprinkle cinnamon lightly all over the parts you just grunged. Place her in the

oven and let her bake until she is completely dry. This will take from 15 to 30 minutes, depending on the thickness of the mixture and oven. Keep checking on her to make sure she doesn't burn. You do not have to flip her over. When she is completely dry, pull her out of the oven and let her cool. All the places you painted with the grunging solution will now be crusty and hard.

4. Sanding. Now the fun begins. Get out your sandpaper and paring knife. If the weather is nice, take your doll outside for this step. If you do it inside, work over your kitchen sink to control the mess. Hold your doll's head in one hand and support her neck, or if you are outside, lay her down on a flat surface. You can even lay her on the ground and work there. Beginning at the lowest place you grunged, sand away, back and forth, back and forth, until the hard layer comes off. Work your way up to her neck.

When you get to the face, take your time, being careful around any floss stitches on her mouth, nose, and eyes. If you sand these too hard, the stitches will come loose. Your goal is to sand off the cinnamon and hard layer of coffee. If you happen to tear the fabric, don't worry. That is all part of becoming a prim. You want that to happen. Keep on sanding until you are satisfied with her appearance.

Be sure to sand all the cinnamon off the doll because through time the cinnamon will turn orange and it doesn't look too appealing. You can use your finger to rub off some of the grunging around the floss without disturbing the stitches. If after all this you still are not satisfied with her appearance, you can always grunge her again. Be very careful with the second sanding. The fabric is more delicate now and more easily torn and distressed.

5. The drawn face. If you have decided on drawing in your face instead of stitching it, now is the time to do so. Since your doll has been grunged and sanded, the pencil marks will remain when you draw her features and you won't sand them off. Don't push too hard with your pencil. You want the doll to look aged, so start lightly, then go back and go over the features a time or two to darken the lines until you are satisfied.

Extreme Prim Face

For my extreme primitive dolls, I take the sharp paring knife and I score her face in the places that I feel will give her extra character, like her cheeks, between the eyes. After I score the face I go back with my sandpaper and sand the torn parts. This will make her look tattered. I love this look—it gives the age-old appearance of a real primitive doll. You can also score and sand spots on the arms and legs to look like worn holes.

This is where rag stuffing really pays off because suddenly you can see the rag stuffing through those holes. I love to see the rag stuffing showing through all the tatters and tears on her now aged face. If you don't want worn holes, skip this step.

Drawn-on face

You've finished the face . . . isn't she something? Notice the holes and tears on her head for that extreme prim look. Now she needs to be gussied up a bit. Let's add some clothing.

CHAPTER 10

Dressing Your Doll

MATERIALS AND SUPPLIES

Fabric of your choice
Pencil
Needle and thread
Floss
Scissors

There are so many possibilities for clothing, both in your choice of fabrics and styles of clothes.

New fabrics

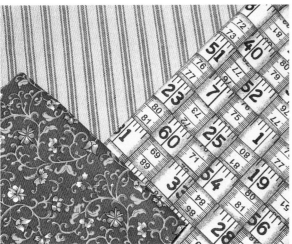

Check out what you can find in a fabric store. Homespun is my personal favorite. It is a cotton fabric with no right or wrong side. Homespun is available in many shades and patterns, solids, checks, plaids, and stripes. Since it is the same on both sides, it is easy to work with.

Calico is another favorite. It is also cotton, but it has a patterned front and is usually cream colored on the other side. Calico comes in every shade and many patterns. I like to mix homespun with calico. I might make a homespun dress and calico bloomers. Look at the quilting fabrics and many other possibilities.

Wool fabrics and tweeds work well, but I would not suggest nylon fabrics. Browse around the fabric store and find what appeals to you.

Cheesecloth is great for aprons or for just wrapping around the shoulders as a shawl. Remember to grunge it first so that it fits the primitive look. It usually comes in a package, not on a bolt like regular fabrics. Grunge up the whole package at one time so you always have some grungy cheesecloth handy and ready to use.

Recycled fabrics

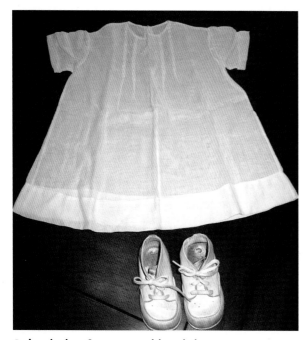

Baby clothes from second-hand shops

Feed sacks make great clothing

How about using old clothing? Maybe you have a favorite flannel shirt but it has seen better days. It just might work for your doll's dress or bloomers. Think about using old blue jeans for overalls for a farmer doll. An old quilt, an old child's dress—you might not even have to make a dress if you design your doll to fit the dress you have. I find old dresses at antique stores and they are usually inexpensive. Feed sacks are wonderful, especially the ones with writing and pictures on them. You can find these online or in antique stores or flea markets. I have even used cloth placemats and old curtains, vintage tablecloths, or linens I've found at garage sales.

How about making a doll that wears a special outfit from one of your children that you have saved through the years? Old bonnets are a great addition—just design the head shape according to the size of the bonnet. I have used just about everything you can think of and there is always a way to make it work. Dolls made with vintage pieces can be stunning one-of-a-kind pieces.

The amount of fabric you need depends on the size of your doll. If you love the fabric, buy some extra to put in your stash for future projects. Usually one yard is enough for clothing for a doll 30" or smaller. If you are making a really large doll, you should have more fabric on hand.

There is no right or wrong way to dress your doll. Sometimes I simply wrap fabric around my dolls and fasten it in place with rusty safety pins or grungy string. Here I'll give you some examples of easy ways to dress your dolls. Try designing your own style dress. Any style is fine because this is your doll and not someone else's pattern. It might take you a few times to get it right, but you are the designer and if you like it, that is all that matters.

Simple dress

Fold your fabric in half, inside out, and spread it out on the table. You will be cutting two of each piece so that you have a front and a back. Lay your doll onto your fabric.

Let's start with a wraparound dress. This is so easy that any beginner can make this one. Lay your doll onto the fabric and have the fabric begin right under her arms. You want plenty of width here so add 5 or 6 inches on either side of her. Then decide how long you want the dress to be. Make a small cut at the length, then tear the fabric across the width that you already marked. Tearing will give the dress a great stringy, unraveled look. Or you can cut the length instead if you want it to be a little neater.

Then match up the outside width edges and simply sew them together with a straight stitch on your sewing machine. I know it looks really wide, but don't worry. Next you will gather it to fit.

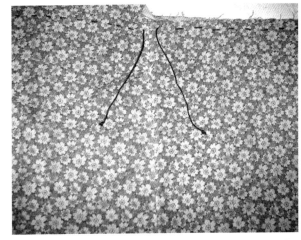

It is easy to do a slip stitch or gathering stitch by hand. I use three strands of black floss (be sure to have plenty of floss on your needle) and knot the end. Start about one inch from the top center of the back of the dress; stitch in and out, in and out, making nice small stitches and leaving plenty of thread behind as you make your first stitch. Stitch all the way around the dress until you come back to your first stitch. Leaving about a three inch tail, cut and knot the thread. Then grab both ends and carefully pull. As you pull, the fabric will start to gather. When it is gathered to your liking, tie it together just like you tie your shoelaces.

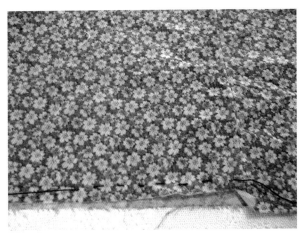

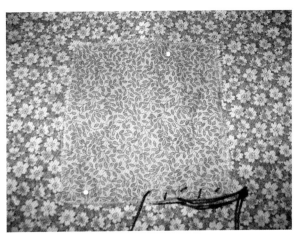

Does she need a patch or two? Cut one out from some other fabric and stitch it in place on the dress. No need to have matching fabrics or even coordinating fabric—anything goes!

So simple and oh, so prim.

Structured dress

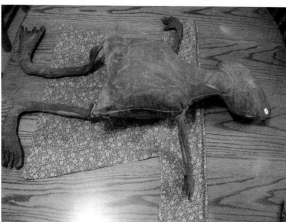

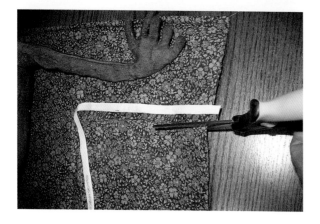

You can also do a regular style dress. Lay your fabric down (remember to fold your fabric in half, inside out, and with the folded side at the top), and lay the doll onto the fabric. Spread her arms straight out, and with your pencil draw the sleeves, leaving an inch or so on either side of her arms. Then moving down with your pencil, draw an angle for the skirt. You want to come out rather wide on each side so her dress will have enough room on either side of her body. Determine how long you want the dress to be. I usually stop right above her feet so her feet will be showing.

Bloomers

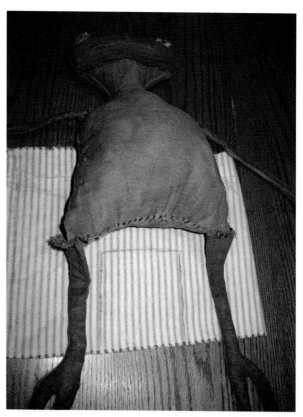

Sometimes I do them, sometimes I don't. I guess it depends on my mood.

Choose a fabric: muslin is nice, or choose a fabric that coordinates with the dress. Here I am using ticking. Fold the fabric in half, inside out, and put the folded edge on the side instead of at the top (this will be one side of the pant leg, the top will be the waistline). Lay the doll on the fabric. One side of the bloomer leg is already complete because the fold is the side of the bloomer leg.

Determine how wide you need the waist to be, and leave an inch or a little more on each side of the waist. With your pencil, draw down the legs, leaving again about an inch on either side of the leg. Go up between the legs, make a "U" for where the bottom of her body is, then go down the other leg.

Assembling the clothing

Once you have both the dress and bloomers drawn onto your fabric, it is time to cut them out. Leave a nice border, maybe an inch or so on each side and cut them out.

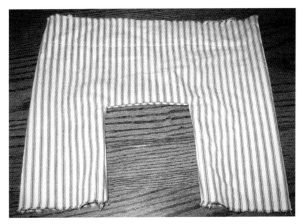

Now you can sew up her clothes. Be careful here: take your time, follow the pencil lines as you sew. You don't have to be perfect and you don't have to sew straight. Just sew it together as best as you can.

After you sew the clothes together, you will trim the seams. Trim carefully, leaving a ¼-inch border around all your stitches. Remember to cut into all corners, sleeves, and the "U" part of the bloomers so that the fabric won't pucker.

Next, turn the bloomers right side out. For long bloomers or sleeves, use the needle nose pliers or hemostat. Remember to use the broken tip pencil to smooth out all the edges.

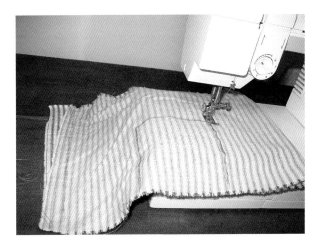

You will have to cut an opening for her head. First you must determine the size of the head opening you will need. Lay your dress down, lay your doll onto the dress, and cut an opening for her head to fit through.

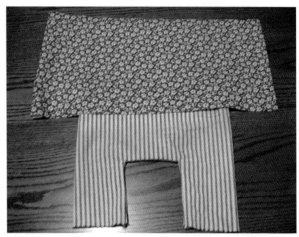

Two primitive outfits for your primitive dolls.

Does she need socks? Yes, you can make socks for her—using real socks. Lay her foot onto the sock you will use and measure just how much you need for the foot length and how high up the leg you want the sock to go. Cut to size, leaving a 1/4-inch border. Sew up the sides (inside out), leaving the top open to insert her foot. You can use baby socks and finish off the look by using baby shoes. Look for old baby shoes at thrift stores or garage sales, the older and dirtier the better.

Grunge the clothing

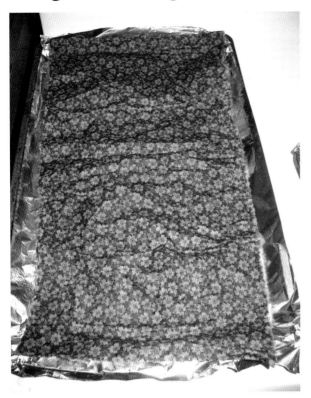

Now you need to grunge the clothes. Prepare the same solution only this time without the cinnamon. (I only use cinnamon to grunge the bodies which will be sanded.) Bring the mixture to a boil. If you have both light and dark fabrics, grunge the lighter fabric first because dark colors often bleed their dye into the solution and can make your lighter fabrics darker than you want them. So start with your light fabrics. Once they are grunged and cooled, lay them on the tinfoil-covered cookie sheet and bake in a warm oven, flipping them over a few times to get an even grunging on both sides. When dry and cool, give the clothes a good sanding. If you happen to tear the fabric that is fine—tears give a more primitive look. Make sure to sand the edges really well if you want that unraveled look. If she has socks, grunge them as well.

Tailoring the clothes to fit

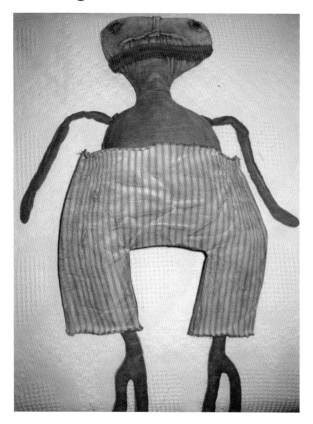

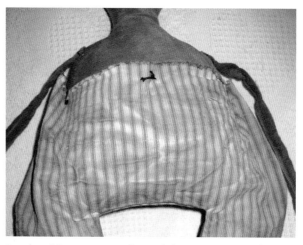

Put her bloomers on first. If they are too wide, then gather the waist to fit the doll. Or use safety pins to attach the bloomers to her body or even string or twine wrapped around and tied tight, like a rope belt.

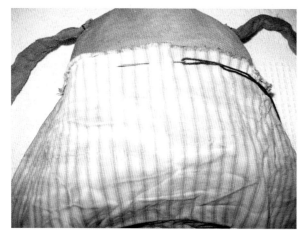

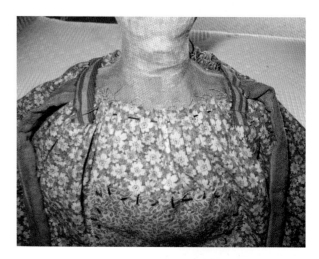

Next slip her dress on. If it is a wrap dress, then slip stitch all around the top of the dress, leaving about two inches of thread on each end to pull tight once you have sewn all around the dress. Now she is dressed.

All the extras

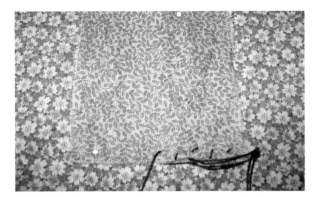

What else does she need? Patches? Sew them onto the clothing, here and there. Fabrics don't have to match and any shape patch will do. Sew them on with tiny childlike stitches—don't bother matching the thread to the fabric because you want it to look old and primitive.

Granny sports a rusty washer necklace

Add other accessories now. Perhaps an old charm, an old key, or a rusty bell on a cord for a necklace. Whatever appeals to you. Slip her socks and shoes on her feet.

How does she look? I imagine that your mind is already whirling with other design ideas. There is no end to the possibilities.

Boots? Add laces if you like.

CHAPTER 11

Hair—Or Petals!

GARDEN DOLL

Hair materials

There are many different types of hair to put on your doll. Believe it or not, my favorite primitive dolls are bald. I like the super primitive look of dolls with no hair. But, as always in the prim world, there are many other choices.

RAW SHEEP'S WOOL

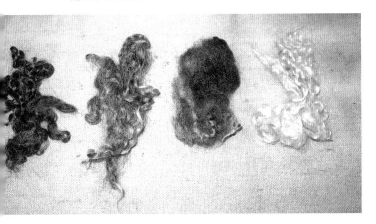

This is exactly what it sounds like: wool straight off a sheep. This comes in a variety of different colors from black to white, and creams to browns, and you can find it in blended colors. Some wool is curly and some is straight; some suppliers brush it for a coarse look. I prefer it not brushed and I love the natural curl in the wool. I find this wool online and when you purchase it from online suppliers, it has most likely been cleaned, which is good. It can be rather pricey but a little goes a long way. If you happen to know a sheep farmer by all means get it locally, but it won't be cleaned and might even be smelly. I have seen it with weeds and seeds and dirt, so be aware of what you are getting.

RAW FLAX FIBERS

Flax fiber is extracted from the bast or skin of the stem of the flax plant. Flax fiber is soft, lustrous, and flexible; bundles of fiber have the appearance of blonde hair, hence the term "flaxen" to describe a blonde. It is stronger than cotton fiber but less elastic.

Raw flax is a personal favorite of mine. You can find it online, sold by the ounce. It is inexpensive and a little goes a long way. It is stringy and easy to work with. Grab a small piece and carefully pull. When you have the length you want, just cut it off. It only comes in one color—a natural cream—and it feels like soft straw and is fun to work with.

COTTON STRING AND TWINE

I use string for more than just hair. It comes in a skein or a ball and can be found just about any-where. I suggest buying only white because it is easily grunged. I love the silly, fun hair it makes. I use string for belts, suspenders, apron ties, and anything else I need to tie up or accessorize. I wrap it around dresses, and I've used it for tails on handmade pigs, cows, cats, and dogs.

I grunge a lot of string at one time. It is simple to do: unravel a whole bunch of string, plop it into my grunging solution, and let it soak for an hour or longer, sometimes even as long as a day. Squeeze out the grunging mixture, put it on your tinfoiled cookie sheet (no need to spread it out flat), and put it in a warm oven to dry. Once it is cool, I put it in a small plastic baggie to store.

Twine is usually found right where you found the cotton string. It is thicker than string, and the strands twine around each other. It comes in a natural color and you can leave it as is or grunge it to get the look you want. After you attach the twine to the doll, you can unravel the ends for a different look. It works well for beards, whiskers, or even pigtails.

Attaching the hair

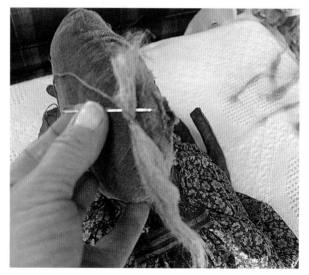

You can use matching floss to attach the hair if you don't want the stitching to show, but for extreme dolls it really isn't necessary. I like to use black floss with flax for my extreme dolls; it shows up really well and emphasizes that it was hand sewn.

To attach sheep's wool: Pull apart as much wool as you want. You can sew it all on at once or sew on little bits at a time. If you want hair that sticks up, then attach it in little bits at a time. With one hand, hold a piece of wool in place on her head and take little stitches. Starting at the back of her head, push your needle through to the front of her head, lay the wool in the center and bring your needle up and over to the back side and again go through to the front. Repeat two or three times, and then knot the thread and cut it. Repeat these steps until you have enough hair on her head and you are satisfied with how she looks.

To attach flax: Use the same method as for attaching wool. You can leave long strands of flax and attach it at the tip of the flax, or you can attach each hunk of flax at the center of the strand. The method you use depends on the look that you want. You can make flax hair any length you like. Sometimes I use a whole lot of sheep's wool and the doll will have the messy "bad hair day" look, other times I just attach a few strands at a time for a more simplified look. With flax fibers, I like to make the hair real messy and have it going every which way for that real primitive look.

To attach string or twine: First of all, decide on the length of hair that you want. Cut the string to length and lay it evenly on her head. Sew the hair on, back to front, up and over from one side to the other and knotting the last stitch. If you attach lots of strands, you can give your doll a ponytail.

Beards for Uncle Sam or Santa are attached the same way, using floss the same color as the facial hair. Pinch together the end that you sew to the doll, and carefully sew it in place under the

Olde Sam

mouth using tiny stitches. Once attached, carefully pull apart the bottom of the beard to spread it out and make it full.

Experiment with different looks. There is no right or wrong way here either; it is just what appeals to you. I don't try to hide my stitches; some artists do, but I feel that if the stitches show, my dolls look handmade.

Petals for a Garden Doll

I've been designing dolls for a long time and I love to get creative and try new looks. For my Garden Doll, I wanted to carry the garden theme straight up to the very top of her head. Why not give her petals instead of hair?

First I cut lots of triangles and sewed pairs of triangles together by hand with a simple back-to-front stitch. I made lots of triangles because I wasn't sure how many I was going to need.

When I had a handful of petals, I held them up to her head to decide just how many I was going to use. The size of the triangles will determine how many you need—larger triangles will mean fewer petals, small triangles will mean she will have a headful of colorful petals.

Then I gave the petals a quick grunging. I painted them a variety of colors to match her clothes and to brighten up her face. I attached the petals to her head using floss, sewing them to the back side of her head, making sure that each petal was sticking up straight and that they were all even.

This look screams "Garden!" and I find it is the prim perfect touch for a spring or summer garden doll.

CHAPTER 12

Must-Have Accessories for Your Prims

COOKING DAYS

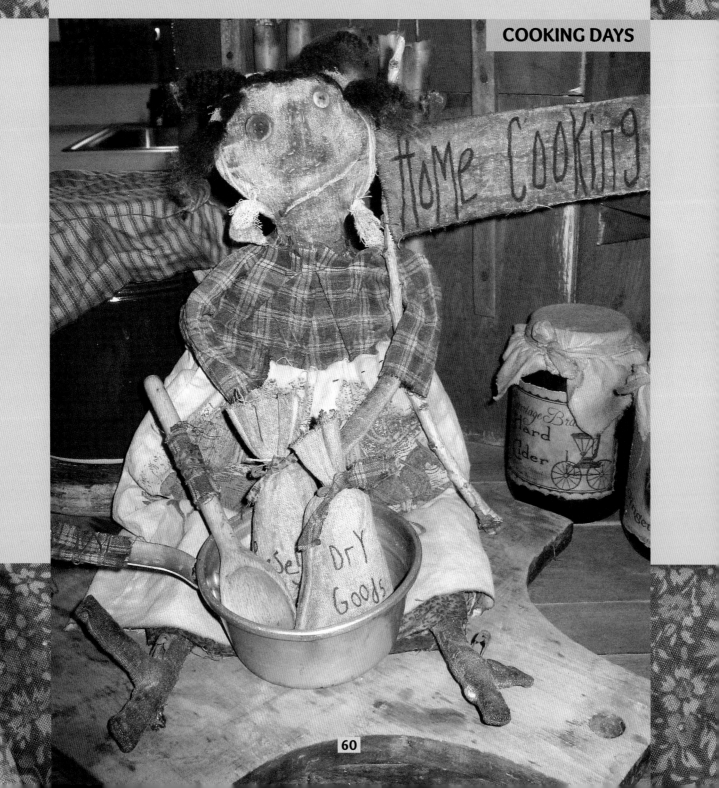

Kitchen and household gadgets

I love to adorn my primitive dolls with primitive accessories, either bought or handmade. Let me describe some of the goods you can buy.

Every once in awhile I need to get out of the house and away from creating. When I can, I head out to an antique store or a primitive shop. As I look around I always keep my eye open for items I might be able to use with a doll. I get ideas for dolls while I am out shopping—perhaps an old garden tool will lead me to think of a garden doll. Little odds and ends and inspiration can be found in the most unusual places. Maybe an old pincushion or a tiny pillow, a little old granny purse, faded pictures from a bygone era that you can insert into a tiny frame, or a piece of vintage jewelry to add to a dress or put in an old jewelry box sitting in her lap. Old primitive kitchen gadgets are great, like rolling pins, sifters, wooden mashers, or a handwritten recipe that was your grandma's, to accessorize a kitchen doll to set on your counter. Knitting needles and an old tin box, wooden bobbins, a yarn ball and paper tape measure, an old pattern and a pin cushion—you have what you need for a little seamstress doll. Unpainted

wooden bird houses from craft stores are great to paint, decorate, and use with a doll.

Think about the possibilities with the holidays. Christmas ornaments for a Christmas doll to hold, tiny little trees or stars, or perhaps a battery operated candle light. Craft stores always have seasonal décor and you never know what item will give you an idea.

Winter means angel dolls. I use rusty wire for the wings and halos. I attach the wings simply by wrapping the wire around her neck and folding the wire to make wings. For her halo, I leave a long piece of wire, like the stem of a flower, and then I wrap the wire in a circle a few times to create the halo. I use a needle to make a tiny hole in the top back side of her head and insert the wire as far down as I can push it.

The possibilities are endless.

Snow Angel

Of course, prim goods can also be handmade by you. Most dolls I create come with a handmade flag—it has become my trademark. I love to make a flag that carries the theme with the doll I make. Flags don't have to be Americana. I use leftover painter's tarps to make the flag part and I gather sticks from my backyard. I like to use cottonwood tree sticks because they shed their branches and they have bumps and nubbies, which make perfect holding spots for the rusty wire I use to hold the flag in place. Some of my flags have writing on them, like "Primitive Blessings" or "Garden Angel" or whatever suits the doll. I even did a doll that was holding a turkey; her flag said, "Eat Pork!" It was one of my most popular dolls.

How about making vegetables, or making a garden rake with a stick and rusty wire. I made a butterfly net using a stick, wire, and cheesecloth. You could make a little pillow and cross-stitch a cute saying or a date on the front. Or give your doll a doll or a baby—it is easy: make a small doll for the larger doll to hold.

Fall and winter: crow, candy corn, tree, pumpkin, candy cane, snowman, sunflower, candy

Spring and summer: eggs, rabbit, flag, carrot, duck, corn, watermelon, green beans

Seasonal goods are also fun: Easter eggs, flowers, and bunnies for spring; Americana flags and veggies for summer; pumpkins and crows for fall; and snowmen and angels for winter. If you plan ahead, you can even make one doll with the intention to change out her accessories with the different seasons.

Draw your own patterns, whatever your doll needs. There is always a way to make it yourself. Remember, what makes these items primitive is that they are handmade and designed by you. You will grunge them just like you did the doll and her clothes. Put them through the same process of painting, grunging, baking, stuffing, and sanding.

Homegrown—and Homemade!— Vegetables

Garden doll primitive goods: carrots, bucket, corn, rake, beans

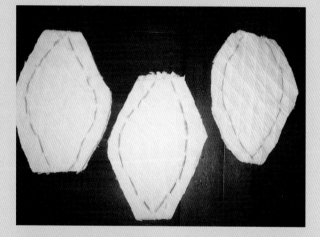

For the corn, I used an old pale yellow chenille bedspread. I cut it into corncob shapes, sewed it up, stuffed each ear with rags, then sewed the top opening closed. Then I grunged the ears of corn and sewed on long strands of raffia and green fabric strips to complete the look.

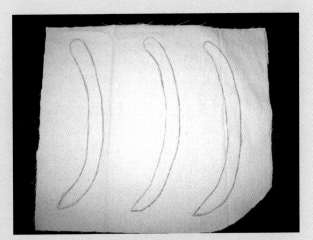

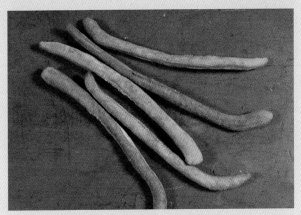

If you make veggies, paint them after you do the first grunging and before you stuff them. After they are stuffed and sewn shut, give them one more grunging, using your paintbrush to apply the mixture. It is not necessary to dust with cinnamon unless you want to. Sand lightly when dry.

For carrots, I cut long triangles of fabric, stuffed and sewed them together, and grunged, painted, and sanded them. I inserted fabric strips for the carrot tops as I sewed the tops closed.

For the green beans, I drew the shapes, then sewed them up leaving a tiny opening in the top so that I could insert the stuffing. I grunged, painted, and sanded them, then sewed closed the little opening in the top.

Pumpkins can have stick stems poked into the top. Sew around the hole to secure the stem; add vines if you wish before you close it tight. Make the vines out of green raffia or wood angel hair vines. (Look for this in the craft store by the moss. It comes in bags just like the green and natural color moss does.)

Experiment and try all sorts of fruits and veggies. Potatoes, onions, turnips . . . apples, oranges, strawberries . . . anything goes when you are making a garden doll.

Prim Flowers for Your Prim Doll

Flowers are a fun accessory for your prim. Draw the shape flower you want on your fabric and very carefully sew around your drawing, sewing two pieces of fabric together for a front and a back. Now cut it out around the sewing very carefully—you won't be able to turn it inside out. Get as close to your stitches as possible.

Grunge, bake, paint, and sand it as you wish.

Find a stick to use as a stem. You can wire the flower to the stick for a primitive look. Poke the wire through the center of the flower: start at the back of the flower, poke the wire through to the front of the flower, then back again to the back side of the flower, bending the wire into a U shape as you proceed. Twist the two ends of the wire together to hold the flower onto the stick.

Rusty accessories

RUSTY WIRE

I use rusty wire on many different dolls. It is great for wings and halos for angels, wrapped loosely around the neck for a necklace or collar around an animal. Use wire for handles for little purses or sacks or to attach a flag to a stick. Rusty wire comes in an assortment of gauges; choose the one that will work well for you. I use 20-gauge because it seems just the right thickness.

I have tried some of the common techniques to rust my own wire, but I can't seem to get it right: the rust never seems to stick. I don't like the smell and it is rather messy. If you try it, be sure to do so in a well ventilated place. Look for instructions online if you wish to try it for yourself.

RUSTY SAFETY PINS AND BELLS

Rusty safety pins can hold the doll's hands together so you can tuck in a prim good. Use pins for a doll's eyes, to gather her collar together for a quick fix if the collar is too wide, or otherwise adjust clothing. Rusty safety pins and bells come in a variety of sizes. I buy all the sizes to keep on hand. A rusty bell strung on a rusty wire makes a cute necklace. Add a bell to the tip of a Santa hat or to animal collars.

CHAPTER 13
The Finishing Touches

Now that you've created this prim, it is time for the finishing touches.

A little bit of fancy?

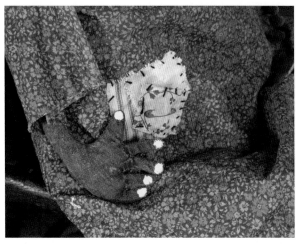

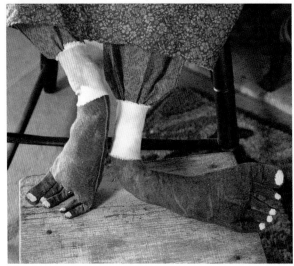

I sometimes add a little rouge to my doll's cheeks or a little lipstick to her prim pinched mouth. Once her face is finished and she has gone through grunging, baking, and sanding, I use a tiny paintbrush and a little bit of a barn red paint, and carefully—with an almost dry brush, after dabbing off most of the paint—paint her cheeks and lips for a little color.

Certain dolls would not be complete without fingernail polish . . . and if she is extra fancy, don't forget her toes!

Shoes for her feet

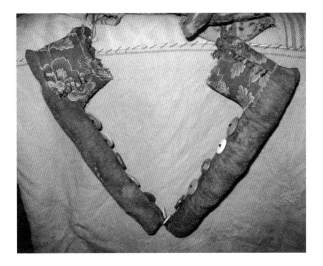

I make many different kinds of feet and shoes and I am always designing new ones. Witch boots with laces are perfect for witches and Halloween characters. Boot-shaped feet are great for Santa and Uncle Sam. Use your imagination.

When you are just beginning it is easiest to stay with simple rounded feet. That is a super-prim style that I love and I still use on my new dolls.

I often use old baby shoes, which I find at thrift stores or garage sales. If they are too clean, I grunge them up with brown or black shoe polish.

Sign your masterpiece

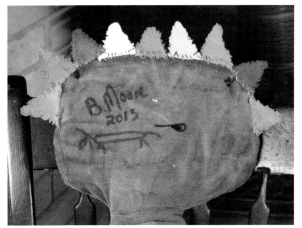

When your doll is all dressed, her hair and face are completed, and her accessories are in her arms, she is looking pretty good. But there is one more very important step: you must sign and date her. She is your creation: take pride in signing her.

I sign and date all my dolls with a fine tip permanent marker. I sign my name and my logo of The Primitive Oswald.

Now, sit back and enjoy your creation

Take pictures of her and share them with your friends. Display her proudly. Sit her in a chair; put her in an old cupboard, in a wagon, on a shelf—wherever you can see her. I have dolls all over my home. They touch my heart and they are conversation pieces.

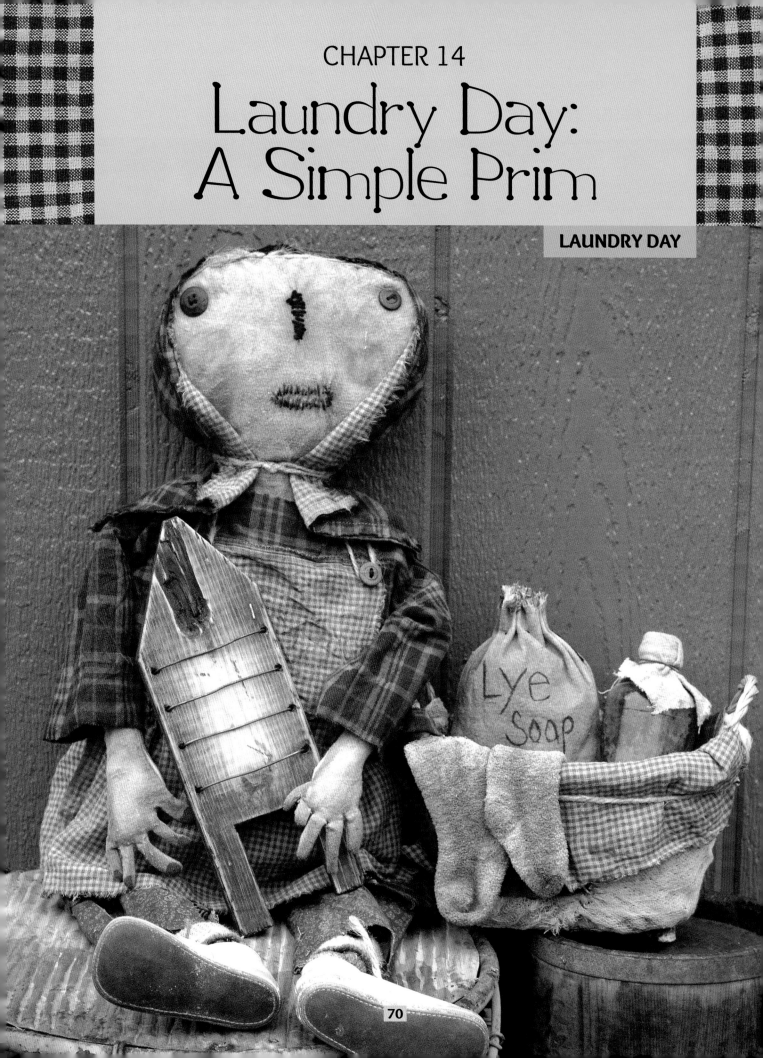

CHAPTER 14

Laundry Day: A Simple Prim

LAUNDRY DAY

When I sat down to design the doll for the cover I was having a hard time coming up with a doll that every person could relate to. My thoughts were scrambled because I was behind on my chores around the house. I kept thinking, "I have so much to do and nothing is getting done." Have you ever had one of those days?

I decided to take a break from designing and get a few things done. I made my way downstairs with my huge pile of dirty laundry and the thought hit me: "Why not make a doll that pertains to me at this very moment in my life?" So my Laundry Day doll came to life.

I decided to make her just primitive and not too extreme. This means I just put her through two stages of grunging and I didn't sand her too much nor did I use my little paring knife to give her tatters. And I didn't paint her. Although she is clearly primitive, she is on the lighter side of prim. This way you can easily see the difference between primitive and extreme primitive.

Her face is just as sweet as peach pie. Her eyes are two old mismatched buttons. She has a simple stitched nose done in black floss, and her mouth is stitched with barn red floss—tiny stitches to look like lips. I gave her cheeks a light blush with barn red craft paint.

Here is how I did it: I used a tiny paintbrush and dabbed it into the paint, then I dabbed most of the paint off. Using a circular motion I swirled the paint onto her cheeks, very lightly; you can always add more if you want a bolder color. If you decide that you added too much blusher, don't worry: when the paint is dry, go back with your sandpaper and, with a swirling motion, lightly sand some of the paint off.

For her bonnet I used long, wide strips of fabric left over from her dress and apron. I sewed them together so that one side was the dress fabric and the other side was the apron fabric. I attached the bonnet with a tiny stitch to the top of her head and then simply tied it on with twine.

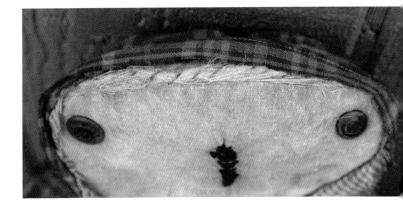

I added just a tiny bit of raw flax fibers for her hair, stitched into place right where her bonnet ends. A simple suggestion of hair that is hidden under her bonnet is perfect for this prim lady.

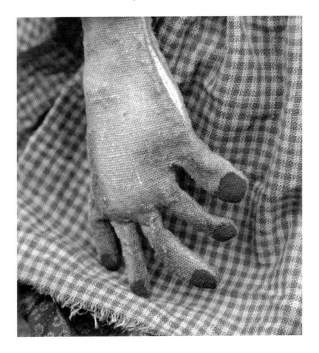

I decided to have some fun with her hands so I gave her red fingernails. This is just one more layer of detail that makes my dolls distinct from other dolls. You can do the same: look for something like that—some small detail—to add to your creations to make them distinctly your own. Maybe you love old jewelry or vintage linens: add an old vintage necklace you found or give her your grandmother's handkerchief. Personalize her with something you treasure.

I knew this lady was a worker, so for her clothing I chose fabrics that appeared to be work clothes. Her bloomers are blue calico, worn and with a few repairs from years of wearing. I "aged" the bloomers by tearing one pant leg just a few inches, then stitching it up again using black floss so you can see the repair.

Her dress is a wool plaid. There are so many wonderful wool fabrics available—have fun looking around and choosing fabric that fits with the color scheme in your home. Her apron is a tan-and-cream checked homespun. None of these fabrics match but they all blend with each other, which creates a mismatched primitive look.

I put some old vintage child's shoes on her feet. You can find shoes at resale shops, flea markets, and anywhere used clothing is sold. If they look too new, just grunge them. These shoes didn't have any laces so I simply used twine.

Her socks were my granddaughter's outgrown socks. When my daughter gave me these socks I knew they were the perfect size for my dolls. If you don't have a new baby around, then go buy some baby socks wherever you can find them and grunge them up.

I gave some thought to the household goods I wanted to put with her. I found a small basket for her laundry supplies—nothing expensive, just a small wicker basket in the shape of a laundry basket. I stained it with dark walnut stain. Then I lined it with grungy cheesecloth, which I wrapped around inside the basket and stitched the ends together carefully with floss on the bottom and sides of the basket. Then I layered the same fabrics I used for her dress and apron inside the basket and made the fabric long enough so it hangs down the sides.

I accessorized the basket with what was needed to do laundry in the olden days. First, she needed a washboard. I made this one using a scrap piece of wood and rusty wire for the rungs. I grunged the wood by staining it with dark walnut stain, then went back over it when it was dry with sandpaper to make it look well worn and heavily used. I found an old dirty brown bottle at an antique store and added a small square of grungy muslin, then tied the bottle in place with rusty wire for the cap. Next I made a fabric bag, grunged it and stuffed it with rags, sewed up the opening using a simple slip stitch, and pulled the ends tight to close it and wrote on it with black marker: LYE SOAP.

I found another old pair of my granddaughter's socks, grunged them up and hung them over the side of the basket—cute little dirty socks ready to be washed. I found some vintage clothespins at an antique store and I grabbed a stick from my yard and wrapped string around it for her clothesline.

There you go: my tribute to the dreaded laundry day. As you can see from this doll, inspiration can come from just about anything.

CHAPTER 15
Prairie Doll: Mother and Baby

PRAIRIE MOTHER AND BABY

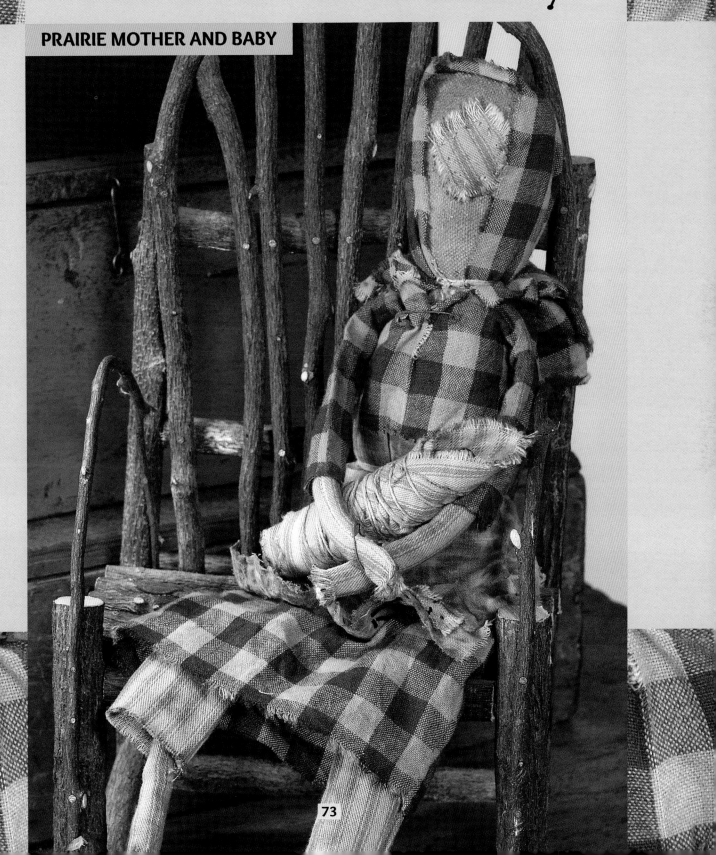

A prairie doll is a certain kind of primitive doll. Prairie dolls make me think of the days of covered wagons, folks traveling to a new part of the country to start a new life, traveling on wagon trains. It was a hard life on the prairie.

Mothers didn't have much to work with and children didn't have many toys. So when a mother wanted to give her children something to play with she did the only thing she could—she made a doll from scrap pieces of fabric and stuffed it with whatever was available. These make-do dolls were simple—nothing fancy, stuffed with scraps of rags, hay, or sawdust. A simple homespun dress, a piece of fabric to resemble a bonnet, and most likely, no facial features would be the finishing touches. These little creations were loved and cherished by little girls and probably had to be repaired many times over.

I wanted my prairie doll to look like she had been loved for many, many years. I gave her face a repair patch, which proves that she has withstood years of being played with and loved. She has a simple dress and a simple scarf on her head, which is attached with stitches on the top and the sides.

I decided to give her a baby. I made this primitive baby from an old clothespin. First I wrapped cotton batting around the clothespin. I was careful to let the rounded top of the clothespin show—that is the baby's head. Then I wrapped fabric over the batting and tied it all on with grungy string.

Prairie dolls can be more involved and fancy if you like that look. You can give her a hand-drawn face. Or you can make her a dress with more details, like a gathered skirt and high laced boots. You could put a little book in her arms. The choice is yours and you can be as creative as you want. Fancy or simple, she is your prairie doll.

A Gallery of Primitive Dolls

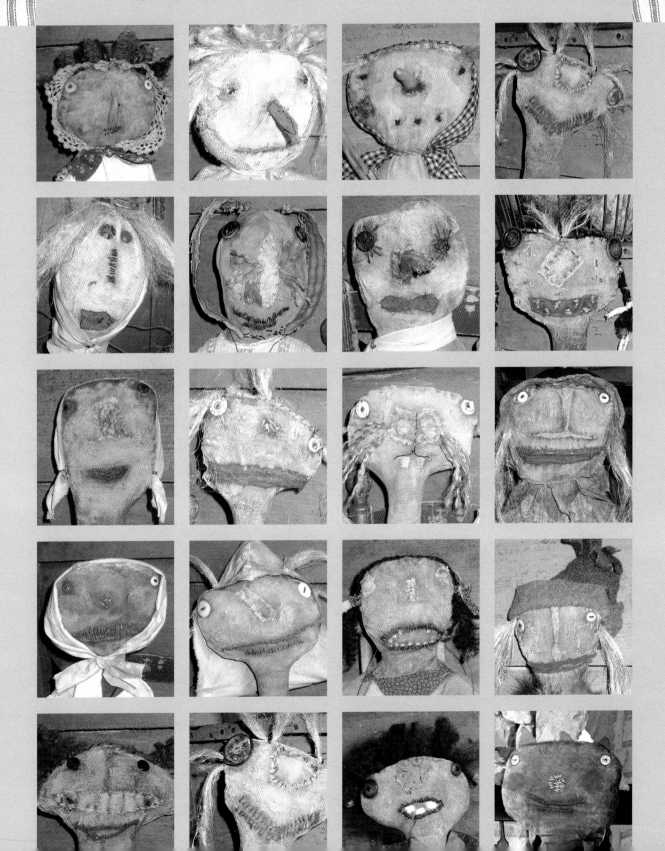

You brought this doll to life, you gave her a personality, and now she will put a smile on your face as she graces your home. She is the perfect primitive accessory and she is a piece of you.

I find that while I am creating I am calm and my thoughts are happy. I lose myself in my work and sometimes that is just what my mind needs. I have created dolls out of heartache and the creative process helped heal my broken heart. Each creation has a special meaning for me.

Sometimes a silliness comes over me and then a silly doll comes to life. It does my heart good to be proud of what my mind and hands have made. So you see, being a folk artist isn't just what I do for a living . . . it is something I need to do. I never thought I could make these primitive creations, but little by little, with many twists and turns and failures and successes, I finally found what works for me.

Take your time; sit and draw what's in your heart. If at first you don't succeed, try and try again. It is a learning process—I sure had to try and try again, and after all these years I still don't always get it right. But that is o.k.

I hope that by following these steps in this book and looking at my work for inspiration, you will be able to create your own doll in your own style. Find your own look: not all prims are like mine. Remember, you are making a one-of-a-kind doll, so no two are ever alike. That is the joy of original design.

So use my drawings for inspiration and ideas, and take off from there. Keep a notepad and pencil with you at all times, wherever you go, so that when an idea strikes you, you can jot it down. I have notebooks full of drawings and I turn to them for inspiration. By now I am sure your mind is racing with the second doll and the third doll and the fourth doll—all those dolls pictured in your mind, and many more to come. Now you have the tools to make as many as you want and they are your very own prims. Take pride in your work knowing that each doll has a piece of your heart in every stitch.

You can do it . . . all you need to do is take the first step.

MR. CHILLS

I'LL BE GOOD!

I'll Be Good

Coal!

OLD LADY MORGAN

PARSON BROWN AND FAMILY

MIZ IDA JANE

GLORIA

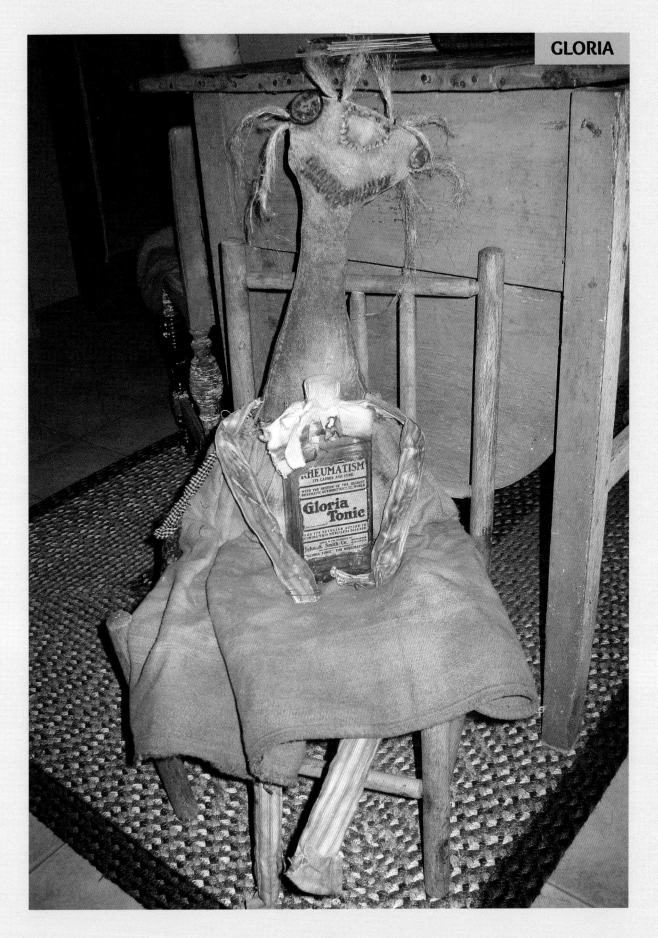

ANGEL

BLUE BUNNY ICE CREAM

BLUE MISSING YOU

HEART AND HAND

HOOT AND ANNIE

OLDE CABIN

PRIM BLESSINGS

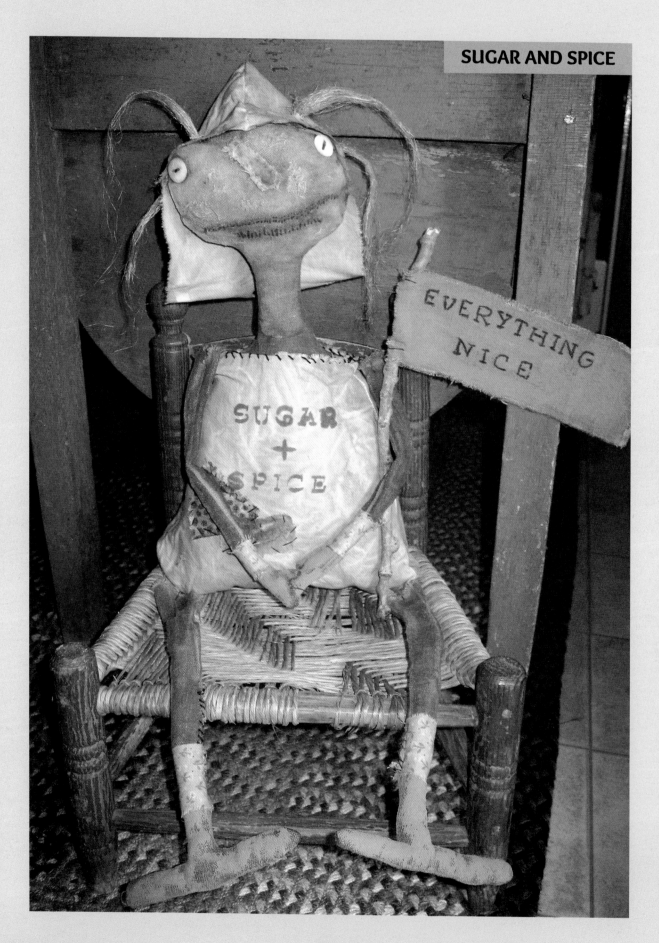

SUGAR AND SPICE

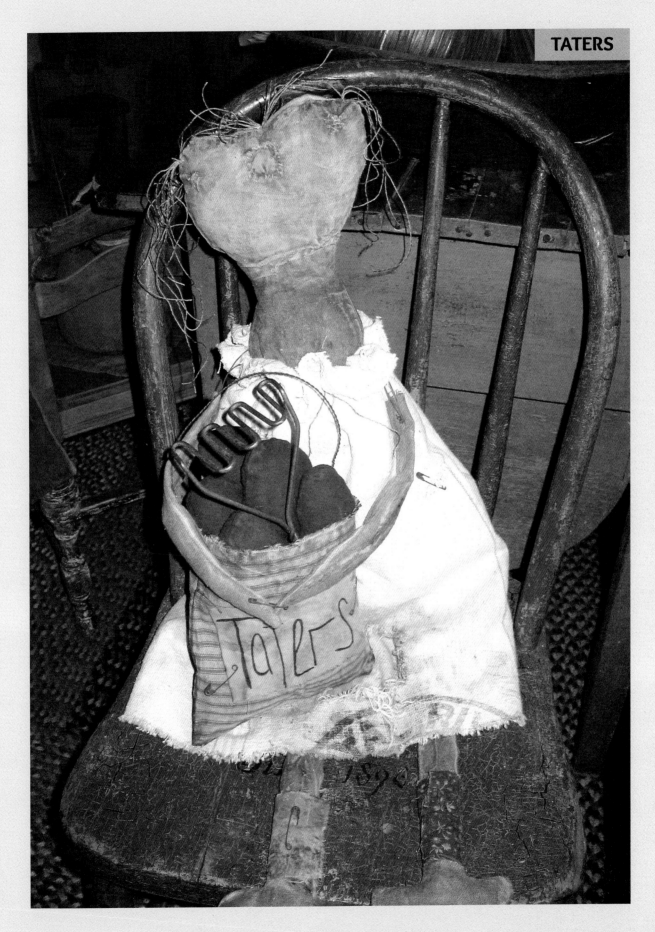

TATERS

TWO FRONT TEETH

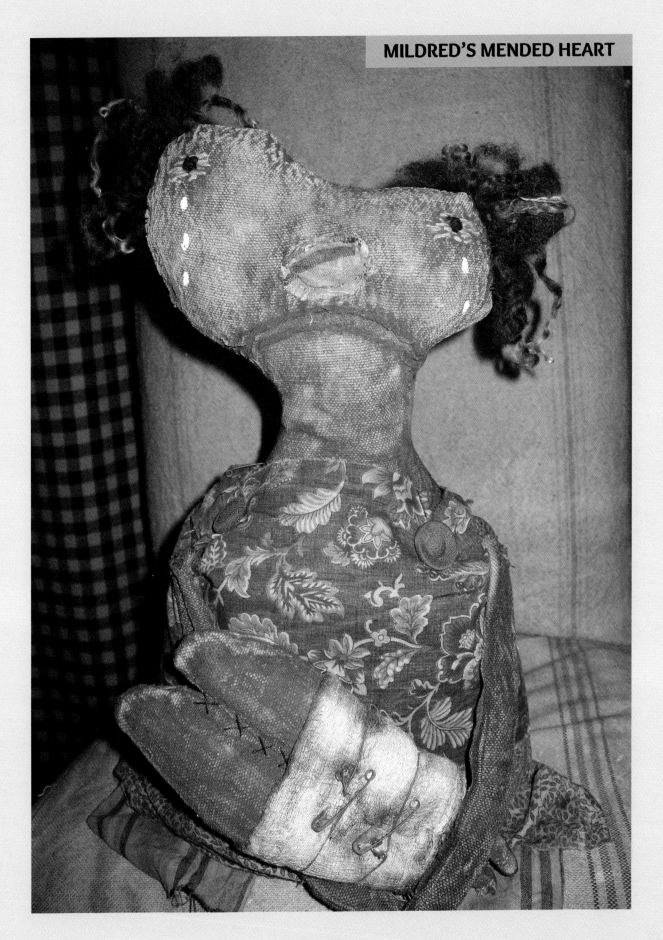

MILDRED'S MENDED HEART

MRS. MAGILACUTTY

HE LOVES ME, HE LOVES ME NOT

PATCHES

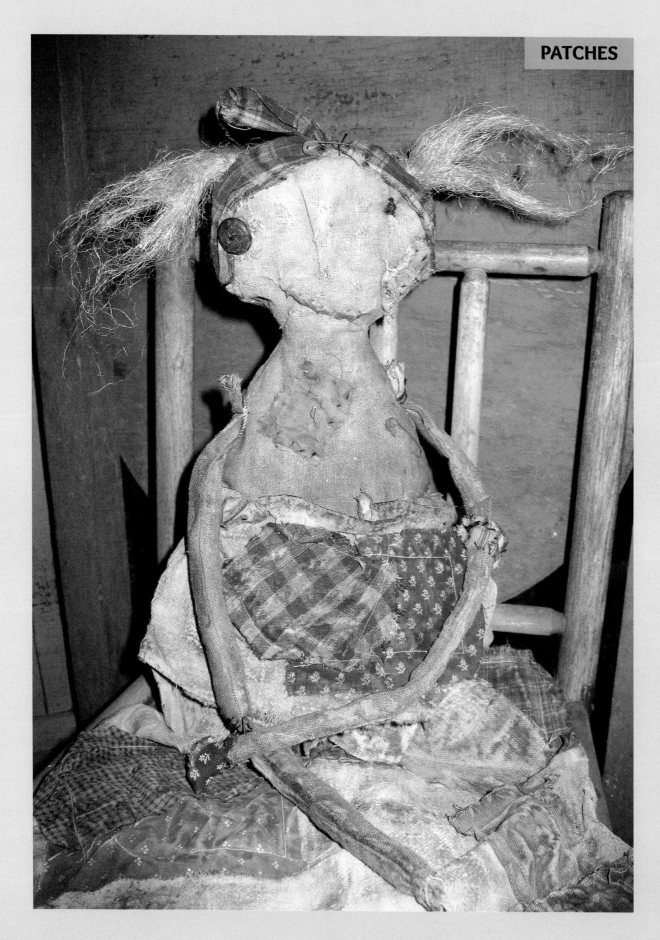

USA

Acknowledgments

There are so many I would like to thank for helping me along this journey.

First, my mom and dad, who taught me to believe in myself.
My amazing husband and children, who have stood by me.
Donna McKinney, who taught me so much and gave me my start
    in creating.
All my customers, who have a piece of my heart in their homes.
Prims magazine, for loving my creations enough to publish them.
Deb Smith, who found a humble folk artist and turned my world
    upside down, and led me in this new direction of sharing what
    I do with others.

To all of them, I give a sincere and heartfelt thank you!

Barb Moore
The Primitive Oswald

The Primitive Oswald